The LIGHT PROCESS

Books by Cheryl Lafferty Eckl

Personal Growth & Transformation

A Beautiful Death:
Keeping the Promise of Love

A Beautiful Grief:
Reflections on Letting Go

The LIGHT Process:
Living on the Razor's Edge of Change

Wise Inner Counselor Books
Reflections on Being Your True Self in Any Situation
Reflections on Doing Your Great Work in Any Occupation
Reflections on Ineffable Love: from loss through grief to joy

Poetry for Inspiration & Beauty

Poetics of Soul & Fire

Bridge to the Otherworld

Idylls from the Garden of Spiritual Delights & Healing

Sparks of Celtic Mystery:
soul poems from Éire

A Beautiful Joy: Reunion with the Beloved
Through Transfiguring Love

Twin Flames Romance Novels

The Weaving:
A Novel of Twin Flames Through Time

Twin Flames of Éire Trilogy
The Ancients and The Call
The Water and The Flame
The Mystics and The Mystery

The LIGHT PROCESS

LIVING ON THE RAZOR'S EDGE OF CHANGE

CHERYL LAFFERTY ECKL

FLYING CRANE PRESS

THE LIGHT PROCESS: LIVING ON THE RAZOR'S EDGE OF CHANGE
© 2013, 2021, 2022 Cheryl J. Eckl, LLC
The LIGHT Process™ | Wise Inner Counselor™

Published by Flying Crane Press, Livingston, Montana 59047
Cheryl@CherylEckl.com | www.CherylEckl.com

All poems are © 2013, except page 144 The Catalyst © 2015.

All rights reserved. No part of this book may be used, reproduced, translated, electronically stored, or transmitted in any manner whatsoever without prior written permission from the publisher, except by reviewers, who may quote brief passages in their reviews.

The information and insights in this book are solely the opinion of the author and should not be considered as a form of therapy, advice, direction, diagnosis, and/or treatment of any kind. This information is not a substitute for medical, psychological, or other professional advice, counseling, or care. All matters pertaining to your individual health should be supervised by a physician or appropriate healthcare practitioner. Neither the author nor the publisher assumes any responsibility or liability whatsoever on behalf of any purchaser or reader.

Library of Congress Control Number: 2013948112
ISBN: 978-0-9828107-4-3 (paperback)
ISBN: 978-0-9828107-5-0 (e-book)

Printed in the United States of America

*There is a light that shines
Beyond all things on earth,
Beyond us all…
Beyond the highest heavens.*

THE UPANISHADS

*For all my teachers.
Yesterday, today, tomorrow,
and always.
You are that light.*

Dear Reader,

There is a story I would like to share with you about *The LIGHT Process*™. This book was originally written in 2013 during a time of truly dramatic change in my life.

I had recently moved to Montana, while my elderly mother remained in assisted living in Denver. Relocating was a tough decision because my mother was quite ill and I was solely responsible for her safety and well-being.

However, the prompting to move had been one of those inner calls to action that I had spent the better part of my life following. So I sold my house in Denver and bought a new one in Bozeman. I moved in on January 11, 2013.

For the next ten months of that year I drove back and forth between Montana and Colorado for my mother's medical appointments and to supervise her hospice care, as she grew ever closer to her transition from this world.

It was during one of those cross-country trips that I hit upon the phrase: *Living on the Razor's Edge of Change*, which aptly described my experience at the time.

The wide open spaces of Montana and Wyoming can feel like the middle of nowhere. The landscape seems very empty, until you start observing the shapes and colors of the land and the sky. Then you may discover that apparent emptiness is filled with life force—and with a choice.

On the razor's edge of change, you can fall into darkness and despair. Or you can persevere to the end of whatever result change is precipitating. When you do, blessings emerge. You may even end up writing a book.

A lot has changed in the ensuing years. But what has not changed is the applicability of *The LIGHT Process*. In fact, the material in this book is perhaps more relevant today than when I wrote it.

Devastating disruptions are hitting faster than ever with greater severity and astonishing global impact. The world may be wired together, but our daily lives are being changed by divisions not seen in recent history.

What are we to do?

The message of *The LIGHT Process* is simple: Stop and ask yourself some questions. Gain a different perspective. Look within for guidance that is always available when you pay attention.

There is a meditative quality to many of these chapters. I find that cross-country travel stimulates contemplation. And poetry. So, the final result of this volume is what I have come to realize is a "philosophy of transitions."

I invite you to spend some time reflecting on the questions, affirmations, stories, and poems. May they help all of your changes be for the best.

Cheryl Lafferty Eckl

CONTENTS

PART ONE: *Reflection*
THE CALL TO CHANGE

CHAPTER 1	Normal Has Changed	3
CHAPTER 2	The Eternally Spiraling Path	10
	Traveling Light	12

PART TWO: *Reconnaissance*
THE ROAD MAP

	Preparation	15
CHAPTER 3	A Guide and an Experience	16
	Heeding the Call	22
CHAPTER 4	The Power of Inquiry	23
CHAPTER 5	The Comfort of Affirmation	27
	On the Way	32

PART THREE: *Resistance*
INTO THE MIDDLE OF NOWHERE

	The Fortress	35
CHAPTER 6	At the Cliff Edge	36
	Paso Doble: Spirals in the Dark	42
CHAPTER 7	A Sign of the Times	44
	The Lament	47

PART FOUR: *Receptivity*
OPENING TO CONVERSATION

	The Bridge at Maam	51
CHAPTER 8	An Invitation and a Choice	53
CHAPTER 9	Hospitality and the New Story (Q1)	59
	Mind the Thresholds	67

PART FIVE: *Reconnection*
WAKING UP AND SHOWING UP

	One Hopes…	71
CHAPTER 10	Waking Up to Inner Truth	72
CHAPTER 11	Creating Emotional Congruence	75
CHAPTER 12	From Coping to Processing	81
CHAPTER 13	Showing Up for Authenticity (Q2)	85
	Brushing the Horse's Tail	90

PART SIX: *Resonance*
A PORT IN THE STORM

	Sean-nós	93
CHAPTER 14	Getting in Sync	94
CHAPTER 15	Listening to the Body	100
	Sensing	106
CHAPTER 16	Between the Unseen and the Seen	108
CHAPTER 17	Into the Fluid Present (Q3)	111
	Spiral Dancing	123

PART SEVEN: *Reconciliation*
HOLDING ON AND LETTING GO

	Silent Song	127
CHAPTER 18	Finding Consolation in Our Memories	128
	Fire Ceremony	135
CHAPTER 19	Releasing the Albatross	137
CHAPTER 20	Viewing Impermanence as Natural (Q4)	143
	Buena Vista	150

PART EIGHT: *Resilience*
BENDING IN THE WIND

	What to Expect from Life	153
CHAPTER 21	Following the Omens	154
CHAPTER 22	Creating a Better Tomorrow	158
	When Things Won't Change	165
CHAPTER 23	Love, Acceptance, and Joy	167
CHAPTER 24	Fulfilling the Heart's Desires (Q5)	171
	The Wild	178

PART NINE: *Renaissance*
THE BEAUTIFUL MIDDLE OF NOW HERE

	Rebirth	181
CHAPTER 25	A Gift from the Divine	182
CHAPTER 26	Be a Traveler, Not a Seeker	185

CHAPTER 27	Making LIGHT of Change	188
CHAPTER 28	A Glimpse of Cosmic Purpose	190
	The Catalyst	194

START HERE GUIDE

If You're in Crisis Now	199

A BIT OF THIS & THAT

Notes	208
Acknowledgements	213
The Conversation Continues	214

Quick Reference for Full Articles About the Five LIGHT Questions

Question 1: *How Have I Been Prepared?*	59
Question 2: *How Am I Staying Afloat?*	85
Question 3: *What Do I Need Right Now?*	111
Question 4: *What Do I Need to Let Go Of?*	143
Question 5: *Where Do I Go from Here?*	171

Affirmations of LIGHT

L   Life has prepared me for my current situation.

I   I practice daily being true to my Self.

G   Grounded in my body, I know what I need.

H   Healing happens when I open up.

T   Tomorrow unfolds as naturally as I allow.

PART ONE
REFLECTION
The Call to Change

*Life belongs to the living,
and he who lives
must be prepared for changes.*

GOETHE

CHAPTER 1

Normal Has Changed

Things are different these days. Everyone feels the shift. There is a tension in the air—a crackling of fluctuation that alerts the senses as it threatens to overthrow the old ways of life.

That's the way of change. "You can't make an omelet without breaking a few eggs," as my mother used to say. Scrambling is certainly what is going on. This new cycle is one that demands unparalleled creativity and innovation amidst dramatic realignment of old frameworks.

Change is welcome when it promises renewed hope and possibility. But *not* when your loved one gets very sick or your job is eliminated. When your house is in the path of a tornado, hurricane, flood, or wildfire, navigating the high seas of volatile events can be a terrifying experience.

Often the biggest casualty of a major transition is our sense of self—of who we are and where we fit into what is euphemistically called the *new normal*. Change is by nature a disruption—even a kind of death. We understand this. The seed must be buried in the ground for the new shoot to emerge and flourish. But we are shocked when our self-identity becomes that seed.

Normality, stability, predictability. These are all elements of a powerful myth that we are in control of our lives. It is an understandable falsehood, because the fact that everything is always in flux can be just too much to comprehend.

So we hold life's overwhelming complexity at bay with action plans and strategies and tactics that work pretty well until things change. Then we are thrown into a literal *Middle of Nowhere*—a place where we are no longer who we were and not yet who we will become.

We tell ourselves that everything will be okay. We'll get through this crisis and come out even better for having endured it. Past experience would say that we're right. But nowadays we're not so sure, because the old ways of surviving major upheavals don't seem to be working as they once did.

Strength and courage and perseverance are still important virtues when dealing with change. But today we must also add to the mix the qualities of gentleness, compassion, collaboration, and humility—even surrender. Most of us don't know how to do that, especially when we're frightened by the new world we see emerging around us.

Normal Has Changed

Twenty-first century change seems to require an almost Zen-like ability to watch and listen for subtle signs that the ground is shifting and then to make swift adjustments that in the past we might have dismissed as superfluous. Now they are critical. In this new environment, *flow* is the watchword of the hour and *flexibility* the attribute of greatest value.

It is no longer sufficient to keep your head down and do your own job. *Don't make waves* no longer applies, because the waves are coming anyway. We had better become more attuned to what's happening or we may be consumed by it.

How many times have you heard about people who, at the last minute, didn't get into a car or board a plane, train, or boat that subsequently crashed? Something didn't feel right, but how did they know?

What about the people who didn't go to work on 9/11 or who stopped for doughnuts or went to an appointment instead of heading straight to the office? Were they just lucky? Or were they following some inner guidance that kept them out of harm's way?

Or what about heroes like Rick Rescorla who had an inner sense that his destiny lay in the path of danger? On that fateful day in New York City, he was not afraid to lose his own life so that others might live. And he did not hesitate to act when his well-schooled intuition compelled him to fearlessly lead 2700 others to safety before the south tower fell.[1]

Part One: Reflection - The Call to Change

Many consider that kind of synchronicity with the cycles of life and death as spooky or superstitious, but we can no longer ignore that the line is blurring between the concrete world we see and the intangible one we cannot.

Learning to bridge those worlds is the need of the hour. Present circumstances are too complex, too volatile, too potentially dangerous for us to simply count on faith or luck. I believe we need to make our own good fortune through conscious refinement of our relationship with the dynamics of the turbulent world we inhabit.

Negative appearances to the contrary, my experience with change has convinced me that we live in a collaborative universe that is ready to help. When we acknowledge its presence and determine to work in partnership with it, the trials of transformation may be mitigated.

The key to that collaboration is the power and presence of the Wise Inner Counselor that lives in every human heart. This internal advocate for Spirit-directed action is the source of our attunement—a fount of limitless creativity, love, and compassion. When we pay attention to its promptings by showing up for life as directed from within, it can also act as the perfect guardian of our destiny—whatever that may be. We may even find joy.

We talk about transitions happening over time or on a continuum. But change is not linear. There is a watery element to the dynamic, but it is not merely fluid. These days it seems as if events are moving at the speed of light. And yet they exhibit tangible cycles that we can work with when we understand that change, like life, unfolds in open spirals, not closed circles.

Each revolution brings us to a freshly created place where both navigation techniques and their application have evolved. Here we are challenged to innovate within established frameworks as well as to develop new ones.

Integration is vital. The new ways must be digested and allowed to percolate through us. And yet, we must also be alert to the human tendency to use a gradual process of integration as a substitute for embracing radical change when that is what's needed.

A slow process isn't effective if we are only sampling change without eating the whole meal. Dramatic events demand commitment—we have to engage.

What we need now is synthesis. Not in the sense of fabricating something synthetic or false, but in collaboratively applying the best of whatever talent or material is available to create a new, multidimensional framework that is uniquely appropriate to the situation at hand.

This is how Nature adjusts to its perpetually evolving environment. It is as if change were constantly creating new webs or crystals of energy—new patterns of thinking, working, and being for exactly this moment, and then the next and the next and the next.

Part One: Reflection - The Call to Change

We can learn to move smoothly through change if we work *with* its flow, not against it. What complicates the process is our resistance to disruption, our doubt that good things can come of the upheaval.

We are afraid that once we open the door to volatility we will never be the same—which, of course, is true. But it is the false self, or ego, that is afraid of losing the empire it has built in our consciousness. The thought of being estranged from its attachments is terrifying. But the point is: One way or another, separation is coming.

Our choice is either to enter into conversation with change and become its partner, or to resist life's demand that we refine our sensibilities. If we hesitate, we may find ourselves embroiled in a worse loss than we see now.

This is not to say that if we are attuned to subtle environmental shifts, unwelcome things will no longer befall us. We live in an imperfect world where tragic events inexplicably occur.

Nevertheless, I am proposing that through the efficacy of inquiry and a willingness to adapt as Nature does, we can enter into a potent relationship with change that can be turned to our highest good and the good we may inspire in others.

In that process, our ability to embrace transition improves. We come into better alignment with the cycles of time and space. And we begin to truly understand what it means to live in the present moment—in that sublime state of awareness where the Middle of Nowhere opens into the Beautiful Middle of Now Here. In that place, we know what to do, where to be, when to take action, even when to be quiet.

Of course, we are still subject to error. Mistakes remain life's most effective teaching tool. But my personal experience with transitions has taught me how to live in that middle place between seen and unseen, earth and sky, past and future—in that realm where synchronicity is the rule, not the exception. This is the razor's edge.

We often catch a glimpse of the truth when taking a sideways glance. So through reflection rather than direction, the goal of The LIGHT Process is to inspire you to create your own multidimensional, ever-renewing spirals of awareness as you flow in partnership with the changes that are bound to appear along the extraordinary trajectory of your own rich experience.

For me, The LIGHT Process has demonstrated that the exact way in which each of us will navigate the spiral remains a mystery. It is not given that we should see much further than the next bend in the road.

And that is enough, because being fully present on that single arc is the key to traversing the great universal nautilus of life itself.

CHAPTER 2

The Eternally Spiraling Path

Each new episode of change thrusts us into a hero's journey, a pilgrimage through the wilderness of ambiguity, where travelers must walk in faith while acting with the kind of resolve that normally accompanies clarity.

Here we must leave the familiar and venture into the Void to confront wild beasts of fear and fierce streams of confusion. Amidst the harrowing storm of uncertainty, we receive support from mysterious guides who appear—often unexpectedly—to lead us over a yawning abyss or even further into the depths.

Here is the crux of the journey, where we must lay aside our defensive weapons and shrug off our expectations. Stripped of all that was useless in body, mind, and spirit, we eventually emerge from the Unknown into a new day of hope and opportunity.

Blinking in the sun of purer reality, our halting steps grow stronger. Imperceptibly at first, we begin to notice

The Eternally Spiraling Path

a lightness of being that would almost belie the perils we have just survived. In a moment of profound connection with something much larger than our self, we are stunned with a realization we never could have imagined: We have become the very Guide who led us through it all.

Somehow this inner advisor's words of wisdom, whispered in our moments of greatest extremity, have taken root and blossomed in our hearts. Almost as if by magic, we now know things we previously could not have known about the past, present, and future.

In the process of losing who we were, we have discovered who we are. We are born anew—more able now to meet a lifetime's challenges and more humble in our awareness that true power lies within apparent frailty.

A vision opens before us. As an eternally spiraling path is revealed, we hear a golden tone. It is a keynote, the sound of our new name—a signet of the transformed being we have become.

Living on the razor's edge of change is now a daily practice. Always perfectly attuned to the present, this new way of being leads us ever onward to more vital and transformative experiences in a finely centered place that has always been right here.

Life has taken on the fragrance of compassion. In the knowledge of what we sense is cosmic purpose, we rest a while, leaning upon the strong oak of divine inspiration—utterly and completely at peace.

Traveling Light

Can I enter the wilderness
    without my stories of the past?

With nothing but a journal,
    a pencil,
    and the knowledge of
    connection beyond the seen?

To journey by the name of traveler
    as an open door
    or a clear pane of glass—

No expectations, no obstacles
    merely hospitable to the day,
    the wind, the rain,

Cloaked only in the belief
    that all is for
    my highest good.

PART TWO
RECONNAISSANCE
The Road Map

*New thoughts are in order
and will emerge
from novel adventures
that open unforeseen doors.*

THE WISE INNER COUNSELOR

Preparation

To commit to the Unknown
    is to open a door
        you didn't know existed.

For Spirit is eager
    for your company
    and rushes in
    to carry you aloft
    into this new adventure
    whose potential you have
    barely just considered.

This way envelops
    one who
    answers the call
    before consent
    is fully conscious.

For the soul knows
    what she's doing
    and packs her bags.

You may as well surrender—
    the journey has begun.

CHAPTER 3

A Guide and an Experience

The LIGHT Process embraces all manner of transition. For those who understand that there is nothing more inevitable than change and who wish to learn and grow in its midst, this work is both road map and inspiration.

For those whose intuition and background tell them that the more dramatic the shift, the more profound the opportunity for deep transformation, The LIGHT Process is both a guide through and an experience of change.

Please note: If you are currently dealing with one of life's seismic events, I suggest that you turn to the Start Here Guide on page 197 to start implementing the essential elements of The LIGHT Process.

Then, when time and opportunity allow, I hope you will return here for a more relaxed exploration of this breakthrough approach to change.

A Guide and an Experience

The LIGHT Process unfolds like an epic tale with multiple scenarios combining to convey a powerfully transformative adventure.

Part One explains why we are called to consider change as the new normal. Here in Part Two, we gain insight into the origin of The LIGHT Process and identify the underlying themes that will inform our travels through volatile circumstances.

Parts Three through Eight are where the action is. Stories, poems, and reflections take us inside the experience of engaging the dynamic energy of change while revealing a multidimensional encounter with transition—a process that leads us out of the familiar into unknown territory.

As we traverse these many layers of self-discovery, we learn to work closely with the inner pilot that I call the *Wise Inner Counselor*—our resident voice of wisdom that already knows how to skillfully navigate a world dizzied by the accelerating pace of ever-changing events.

Part Nine is the final leg of our journey that unifies all parts into a state of consciousness I call the *Beautiful Middle of Now Here*. This level of awareness emerges from our passage through uncertainty and then prepares us for the next cycle of transition.

For if there is anything we *do* know for certain, it is that life does not stand still. How to effectively meet the challenges of fluctuation is the task before us.

Part Two: Reconnaissance - The Road Map

The LIGHT Process encourages those who have been profoundly affected by change to engage the process of transition rather than trying to speed through it. And it offers practical suggestions for those who by choice or chance often find themselves on the front lines where everything is in flux. As one who has spent much of her life on that razor's edge, I know that the process works.

Origin of The LIGHT Process

It seems as if The LIGHT Process has been pursuing me for decades. Both personally and professionally, it has percolated through my life, offering ever deeper insight into how the world works, executing its transcendent magic at every level of my being.

It all began in my early teens when my first musical theater roles introduced me to that sublime realm of creative spontaneity that sparks to life on stage. I thrived in that space where anything could happen—and often did. It was like flying without a net, and I loved it.

Although life propelled me out of the theater in my late twenties, new frontiers have always been close at hand. I have often sought change for its own sake, gaining fresh perspective while engaging new challenges.

And over the years, I have made dozens of dramatic moves because it was the right thing to do at the time. A cycle was complete, there was nothing left for me to accomplish, and I knew it was time to move on.

A Guide and an Experience

Not surprisingly, I have often found myself at the center of departmental or organizational restructuring. It is as if some unseen force sends me into situations that have recently shifted to help facilitate the transition from one form to the next. And if things haven't changed yet, the status quo tends to get wobbly when I show up.

My more intentional and personally transformational relationship with the razor's edge began when I was employed as a management instructor/facilitator for a large training company on the East Coast. The organization's approach was to create an emotionally safe and intellectually open classroom environment in which students could arrive at their own insights through discovery activities and group discussion.

The preferred facilitation method relied heavily on inquiry. The course that made the best use of this technique was on critical thinking and creative problem solving. It was my favorite teaching event because it attracted a good mix of concrete and imaginative thinkers, which was both interesting and a challenge.

In my early days as an instructor, facilitating the differences between attendees' perspectives and preferences was like surfing giant waves. I never knew what was going to arise in the discussions. But after a while, I learned to relax and listen acutely to the promptings of my own Wise Inner Counselor. When I allowed this improvisational spirit to guide what I said and when I said it, the

Part Two: Reconnaissance - The Road Map

experience was more exhilarating than any stage performance. Facilitation became like dancing with a force that I soon identified as the divine within me.

One of the most important lessons I learned about critical thinking and creative problem solving is that we do a better job of each when we stop and ask some questions to clarify what we are trying to accomplish.

When my husband became ill and subsequently died of colon cancer, this process of mindful inquiry spilled over into my personal life. At the peak of our worst days, when he was getting sicker and I was still traveling for work, I asked myself dozens of questions in an attempt to figure out what was happening and what to do next.

Eventually, the essential five questions morphed into what is now The LIGHT Process.

Philosophers have posited multiple dimensions of reality. Meditation masters have identified many planes of elevated consciousness to which the human psyche has access. I believe that dynamic change also involves numerous levels of awareness.

We can explore them as states of mind, stages of personal development, or contextual themes that describe the phases of transformation we experience in our travels through life. Regardless of the model we follow, at some point we will likely realize that our

A Guide and an Experience

seasons of existence on this earth are more than merely repetitive cycles. In fact, they are continually evolving with rich and complex possibility.

As we explore the interior aspects of change, we discover that it operates more like a spiral than a circle, with each revolution holding the potential for improvement over the previous one.

We also see that the process is inclusive as well as creative. Each succeeding turn of the spiral builds upon what came before, retaining as well as reframing themes from its predecessors. When we pay attention, these contextual elements can act as signposts to help guide us through volatile events.

So far, the themes I have identified are: reflection, reconnaissance, resistance, receptivity, reconnection, resonance, reconciliation, resilience, and renaissance. For the purposes of this book, each numbered section pertains to a single theme.

The LIGHT Process can be deeply personal and profoundly self-renewing as we respond to the call to change. The essential task for each of us is to actually hear that call and then answer it.

Heeding the Call

A well-tuned heart
Brought you to this place,
But a new song is playing.

What you heard before
Was merely prelude.
The orchestra invites you
To notice the difference.

CHAPTER 4

The Power of Inquiry

Emotions can run high in the early phases of transition, rendering clear thinking improbable and practical options invisible. It is while swamped in this maelstrom of confusion that we most need a lifeline—and that single rope of clarity is inquiry.

When someone is angry, we don't yell at them, "Calm down!" That only inflames them further. Likewise, when someone is in the throes of change's deep waters, we don't tell them to "get a grip" or "get over it."

Platitudes are insulting and certainly ineffective. Conversely, a well-placed question can begin to shine a light into the darkness, offering a single step that can be followed by a second and a third.

Arnie's Story

Inquiry operates a bit like the story of Arnie, a donkey that stumbled, fell, and landed at the bottom of an abandoned

Part Two: Reconnaissance - The Road Map

well. He was wedged too tight for a rescue. Block and tackle wouldn't fit. There was no way to haul him out, and donkeys don't climb vertical walls.

His owner, Ike, was desperate for a solution. Amidst the donkey's plaintive braying and his own anxiety over the probable demise of his beloved beast, Ike asked himself a question: *What if I could raise Arnie from the inside out?*

Grabbing a shovel, he dug up a small amount of dirt and threw it down into the well. Most of it landed on the donkey, who must have wondered why he was being further abused.

Arnie shook off the dirt, stamped his feet, and looked up at his owner, who was peering hopefully down at him. "Good boy!" cried Ike. "Shake it off!" And then he tossed in another shovelful of dirt. Arnie shook again, looked up, and was once more praised for his actions.

Soon the light dawned, and both the man and his donkey spent the next several hours shoveling, shaking, and stamping as the floor of the well rose steadily skyward. Eventually the dirt was high enough for Arnie to simply walk out on his own four legs.

This story explains how inquiry can guide us out of a deep well of misery. It not only provides a new, more solid foundation for what comes next; it also helps us move out of emotional reactions and into practical actions.

When dealing with transitions—either those we choose or those thrust upon us—inquiry is the agent that paradoxically accelerates our ability to effect positive change by inviting us to stop for a moment and take stock of what is transpiring.

When our heads are spinning, taking time out to catch our breath and ask five simple questions can make all the difference in the outcome. People who are expert critical thinkers and creative problem solvers do this naturally. The rest of us may need a guide that separates the process into its individual parts so we can explore them one by one.

Then, having once consciously traversed the spiral of change, we are better equipped to more quickly complete the next journey when it occurs—perhaps even in that millisecond of in-breath between thought and action.

When that happens, we know we are living on the razor's edge.

When everything that was familiar seems to be passing away, inquiry is an effective way in which to reframe the amorphous nature of the unanswerable *Why did this happen?* into a more concrete *What happened?* or *How shall we deal with it?*

As we will see, much of The LIGHT Process is really an exercise in re-envisioning the overwhelming as

Part Two: Reconnaissance - The Road Map

the possible. As we divide massive changes into smaller increments that are guided by five easily remembered questions, we start to feel powerful.

Our new life begins taking shape. And ultimately, we find meaning, peace of mind, and a way to help others.

CHAPTER 5

The Comfort of Affirmation

Effectively used, positive affirmation is much more than happy talk—although it can feel rather simplistic when we are in the throes of uncertainty.

Doubt is a formidable adversary, especially when all we see is darkness. In the deep waters of emotion, it is difficult to believe that the light will ever dawn.

In that hard place, positive affirmation can taste like so much psychological cotton candy or what author and psychologist John Welwood calls *spiritual bypass*—using spiritual techniques to stay in a magical, happy place instead of engaging all of life, shadows as well as light.[2]

In the case of unwelcome change, or other people's resistance to the restructuring we may have initiated, sometimes we just have to dive in, take the next step, and work with it until the positive outlook emerges. This process can take some time, because we may have to act as if we believe what we're professing until we actually do.

Part Two: Reconnaissance - The Road Map

I learned that lesson during my years in the entertainment industry. "The show must go on" was very real to me. I have gone on stage with a 104-degree fever, a lacerated foot, and laryngitis. Not all at the same time, of course. But the point is that, in each case, I acted as if I felt great until I did.

Almost nothing is as contagious as a smile. So when the audience watched me giving an upbeat performance, they reciprocated—mirroring that happy expression back to me, boosting the energy I needed to finish the show.

Desperate times create the same equation, only now we are dealing with a cosmos rather than an auditorium full of people. In my experience, the Universe is no less generous than the audiences of my theater days. Of course, I still have to do the work, but I have found that there is something about affirming my ability to achieve a successful outcome that makes the labor less daunting.

Another important function of positive affirmation is its ability to shield us from the toxic what-ifs of what we call *catastrophizing*. These irrational thoughts that something is far worse than it really is can erupt in the midst of changes great or small. Even otherwise stable personalities can fall under its spell.

When our lives have been disrupted by external forces, affirming our ability to flow with circumstances can help dispel the understandable notion that the sky is falling or that even more catastrophic events are right around the corner.

When we are the ones initiating change, we may be subjected to the frightened imaginings of those who feel threatened by our plans. Friends, family members, employees, or colleagues may not share our vision for the future. As agents of change, it is important for us to bring them along with compassionate understanding of what we are asking them to adjust to or give up.

Simply telling those concerned that everything will work out fine is not an appropriate use of affirmation. It is our responsibility to explain to others what we expect to change and how we plan to go about making that happen.

In these situations, positive affirmation is a personal activity. We use it to bolster our own confidence and to maintain an open, engaged attitude toward those we wish to include in a collaborative approach to transformation.

The key to anchoring positive affirmations is to combine them with focused visualization of the uplifting circumstances we are invoking. Sometimes creating a vision board[3] that conveys the *felt sense*[4] of our goal can encourage us toward a transformative future that even unwelcome change invites us to consider.

A highly effective way of encouraging mutual transformation is to invite a group that is involved in change to create a shared vision. The insights that emerge and the enthusiasm that is generated in such an exercise can continue to stimulate ongoing progress with remarkable effectiveness.

Affirming Our Highest Intentions

Once only the purview of the religious, nowadays using the words *I am* to bolster positive affirmation is a practice accepted by spiritual and personal growth practitioners around the world.[5]

Many twelve-step programs and life coaches have applied this technique for years, encouraging their clients to use statements such as *I am in perfect health* or *I am successful* or *I am talented, courageous, and wise* as part of their journey through personal and professional development.

I have found affirmation to be an effective method for flipping questions that imply lack or negativity into abundantly positive statements. *Why me?* can morph into *I am the perfect person to deal with this challenge.* Planning for the future can shift from *Where do I go from here?* to *I am being called forward to a bright new tomorrow.*

Once we learn to pay attention to the content of our own inner conversation, changing the flavor of that dialogue by using *I am* followed by a positive affirmation is a skillful way to enhance self-discovery.

And because the words *I am* refer to the Divine, we reserve their use for stating our highest intentions. As one of my teachers explained, the words *I am* unleash spiritual energy that flows into situations according to how we state them. So if we want to improve our circumstances, it is more useful to couple the divine name with a positive statement than to reinforce an idea of scarcity, depression, or ill health.

The key here is to combine our *I am* statements with correspondingly uplifting feelings—the felt sense—about what we are trying to accomplish. For example, if I affirm *I am in perfect health* but I focus on how dreadful I feel, I may be setting myself up for mixed results. However, I can improve the statement and the likelihood of regaining my vitality by saying, *Every day I am taking steps that bring me closer to perfect health.*

This takes affirmation out of the realm of wishful thinking and places it firmly in the arena of positive action. Engaging the divine name makes the process even more vibrant.

For example, we could say, *Life has prepared me for my current circumstance, and I am able to meet the challenges that come my way with poise and a clear head.*

On the Way

Out of the questions
That guide me through the Unknown
Answers emerge filled with encouragement,
A reminder, and a key—

The journey flows through light.

PART THREE
RESISTANCE
Into the Middle of Nowhere

*Human beings do not go hand in hand
the whole stretch of the way.
There is a virgin forest in each;
a snowfield where even the print
of birds' feet is unknown.*

*Here we go alone, and like it better so.
Always to have sympathy,
always to be accompanied,
always to be understood
would be intolerable.*

Virginia Woolf

The Fortress

Encircled 'round opposed the gale
The tempest hard upon the keep
The forecast called for sudden squalls
Appearing o'er the ramparts.

No cracks just yet, the castle held
We knew the blast was coming
But citizens quaked at sight of this—
A storm unlike the others.

The watchman cried,
"Look east! north! south!"
The west wind was the strongest.
The tower shook, all rigid brick
No safeguard 'gainst the whirlwind.

In one great crash our walls came down
While trees bent low, but did not break
The stronghold fell despite its strength
Our bulwark was illusion.

CHAPTER 6

At the Cliff Edge

There is something in us that understands what Virginia Woolf meant about the intolerability of being "always understood." We take offense when somebody declares, "Oh, I know just how you feel" or "I know exactly what you're going through." How dare they presume!

I expect the Universe feels the same. Change offers an opportunity to explore but it is not the promise of perpetual clarity. Eternally true to itself, the Unknown remains unknowable. It defies a frontal assault. And we who would penetrate its secrets suffer most when we fail to honor its privacy.

Woolf knows that we are compellingly drawn to mystery. And yet, we also resist it. When change hurls us to the cliff edge, we shrink back. The darkness is so much bleaker than we expected. So we suffer. We complain. We doubt that anything good will ever come of such hardship and isolation.

However, we also know that life would lose its savor if every mystery were solved. So, experiencing resistance to change can be a useful messenger that alerts us to our fear of ambiguity. It is natural and understandable—and yet, we must persevere. As my Wise Inner Counselor told me years ago:

> *Do whatever you need to bolster your courage for the wilderness experience of the Middle of Nowhere while also ensuring that you do not avoid it. Sugarcoating the intensity of how lost you feel in the early phases of dramatic change is no way to engage it.*
>
> *Mastery is found at the summit. Cowering in the lowlands of resistance gets you nowhere. When and how you make the trek to the razor's edge is up to you. Just remember: In a self-actualized life, the journey is not optional.*

Like the steady beat of "The Fortress," the drumbeat of the future portends uncertainty. Resistance is futile, yet we strain against the unknown anyway. We can't help it. It's how we are wired to respond to what's different.

Political correctness and diversity training aside, our brains are designed to detect the unfamiliar, labeling it as "other" and a threat. They persist in this opinion until we can analyze the situation and convince our fight-or-flight reflex to stand down.

This whole sequence happens in a flash of pattern recognition, comparison, and release. And in that instant, huge amounts of adrenalin and other powerful hormones are pumped throughout the body.

Leg muscles tense to facilitate flight. Eyes widen and scan the horizon for looming threats. Fists, jaws, and abdomen clench in anticipation of body blows. Digestion shuts down to shuttle blood to the extremities. And higher-order thinking processes take a backseat to primitive responses that have historically supported physical survival in dangerous environments.

When the threat subsides, so do the hormones, although the body will need the assistance of some type of stress-relief activity to complete the process. If we have become emotionally upset during the perceived attack, it can take even longer for us to return to our right mind.

Severe stress response that causes post-traumatic stress disorder (PTSD) may require months or years to resolve—and then often only with the assistance of a therapist skilled in treating the physical (somatic) residue of trauma.

If you or someone you know is dealing with PTSD or complicated grief brought on by traumatic loss, I would encourage you to read the classic work *Waking the Tiger*, by Peter A. Levine, Ph.D.

Levine is an American therapist, author, and educator who specializes in the understanding and treatment of

PTSD. Through the skillful application of his techniques, persons who have suffered trauma can find relief. They may also discover welcome explanation for why their stress-related problems have resisted treatment in the past.

Many healthcare practitioners do not realize that even mild forms of trauma are characterized by somatic energy that was not discharged after a real or perceived threat. It is most likely this residual energy that caused the affected person's body to respond with multiple and persistent physical as well as emotional symptoms.

With trauma, we quite literally have "issues in our tissues." Talk therapy is largely ineffective. In fact, talking about a terrifying event can actually re-traumatize the victim. Thus, the energy has to be physically discharged; and to do this effectively requires skill.[6]

Even without a traumatic experience, when the perception of threat persists, as it tends to do in our modern world, so do the symptoms of heightened awareness. *En garde!* becomes our continuous state of fearful defiance as we brace against the winds of change that threaten who or what we hold most dear.

Maintaining these mental, emotional, and physical barriers against a perceived enemy is exhausting. Yet the resistance is understandable. Fear of what is unknown makes sense.

Part Three: Resistance - Into the Middle of Nowhere

However uncomfortable the present difficulty, at least our coping mechanisms are familiar and well practiced. We have developed a more or less successful pain management system and we know—or at least we think we know—who our friends are.

The fear of unbearable pain and suffering is surpassed only by the fear of death itself. And if the underlying source of resistance is fear, one of its most destructive manifestations is guilt.

Perhaps you are familiar with some of its voices: *What will we do without you? Who do you think you are? We tried that once and it didn't work. You'll be sorry. If you loved me, you'd stay. I can't leave now; they're depending on me. They'll never forgive me. I'll never forgive myself.*

One of the most troubling feelings in the Middle of Nowhere is that of isolation. Whether change stems from outer forces we cannot control or from an inner calling to escape the status quo, we become separated from our peers.

We don't know where we belong in relation to others. We no longer fit with the old club and the new one may not yet be apparent.

Or, if we do have a sense of the group we want to join, the existing members may have rejected our application. So the unwelcome seatmates of guilt and fear contribute to the sense of extreme vulnerability we take with us into the Middle of Nowhere. Like it or not, this is the unavoidable wasteland into which we must venture if we are to come out the other side of circumstance as the transformed creatures that, at this point, our minds cannot conceive.

And yet—some internal mystery of our own vibrates with the sense that the trek through the wilderness is worth the effort. Something in us is compelled to challenge the fortress of resistance we have constructed against the very answers we seek.

This is the voice we follow over the cliff edge into uncertainty.

Paso Doble: Spirals in the Dark

"It's safe in here," she says to herself.
"The door is locked, the windows barred,
    no way for the creature
    to gain entrance
    to my sanctuary."

Lotus-posed, she seals her peace
    with chant and charm—
    impervious at last.

Ears stopped, shields up,
    lest the howling without
    jar her careful quiet.

But what knock has howl become?
What pounding now
    that her studied protection
    will not drown?

"Be still!" she shouts.
"You are not welcome in my den.
Have you no respect for sorrow?
A minute's peace is all I ask.
Why won't you go away?"

A breath, a beat, a space, a pause—
And then a curdling cry
    that shakes her house
    to its foundation.

"Too much, too much," she bleats.
"You've pushed me far enough!"
Irate, door flung open, windows ajar,
    eyes wide, ears perked,
    looking out, surprised—
    at nothing after all.

Slowly she closes the door.
Latches, locks, and shutters the portal
    in satisfied relief.
Then turns with sudden shock
    into the face of two fierce eyes
    glowing gold
    behind the snarling snout
    that threatens to devour her.

Circling 'round each other now,
    never breaking eye contact,
    they move first left, then right
    in ever-tightening spirals.
Closer and closer
    until he rises up
    and snatches her to his breast—
    not into his glistening maw,
    but to his heart in wild embrace.
And to her great astonishment—
    they dance.

CHAPTER 7

A Sign of the Times

Some time ago, a friend sent me an e-mail describing his personal experience with the Middle of Nowhere. The clinic where he had worked for years was closing and he suddenly found himself adrift in rough waters.

With his permission, here are some of the stunning points he made from the thick of having his world turned upside down:

> Everything seems to be changing, at a rate faster than the will or intellect can keep up with.
>
> Not entirely a surprise, but a shock nonetheless. This is a change far-reaching in its effect.
>
> So there is a great deal of grief. We are all wounded deeply by this turn of events.
>
> I wonder: Do I really want to keep beating my brains out for an agency, relatively low pay, and the security of a paycheck and health insurance?
>
> I feel a fragmentation of my own path coming on. Perhaps some breathing space for doing some research

A Sign of the Times

and writing. Don't know yet how it will turn out.

If I sound passive, it's because I feel that I have no control over events, not even of the interviewing and hiring process.

I feel as if God is calling me to pass through the eye of a needle, and that I have had to drop, piece by piece, all the encumbrances that would prevent that narrow passage.

There's a lot of self-reform in that, mostly in surrender, in a sense that the variables of things at this time are far too large for my own small mind to encompass, and therefore I find an increasing reliance on Spirit as a guide.

I have had in the past two months the clearest and cleanest realization of faith I have ever had, and also the most tortured sense of terror and darkness.

Some of the things I need to drop [what he calls his "inferiors"]: anger, resentment, hatred, wounded pride, fear, self-condemnation, and so forth. These are the things I don't need to pass through the needle's eye. In fact, I can't pass through it with all that baggage.

Tares and wheat—what do I need for the journey?

It's the finding of a complete trust in God in the face of all concrete facts arguing against it and the argument in the voice of my inferiors that I must DO something NOW!

I have been given another picture: Sign of the times, and a need to wait, and to preserve my character and dignity while waiting. And this with the full faith—a kind of knowledge—that the dark time will pass away.

So it is an exciting trial.

Part Three: Resistance - Into the Middle of Nowhere

My friend's vivid description resonates with my own experience of the Middle of Nowhere that occurred while I was on a powerfully transformative pilgrimage one summer in Ireland.

My soul has a profound connection to the land of Éire and I love the place. And because I am so open to its mystery, I find that the energetic record of its centuries of suffering unfailingly impinges upon my consciousness.

So despite eventually contacting the deep, ancient spirituality of its "thin places"—where the veil between this world and the next is said to become transparent— each time I visit Ireland I also touch upon the despair of its population, long and persistently thrown into chaos by outside forces.[7]

The following poem, "The Lament," is my depiction of that emotional hinterland, written in the midst of a particularly Irish version of the Middle of Nowhere.

The Lament

The middle of nowhere is not beautiful.

Dank, dark as wet limestone,
    treacherous in its secrets,

Ready to swallow all your
    hopes and dreams
    in a moment of
    smug inattention

The millisecond before the
    ground you knew,
    or thought you did,
    gives way with sudden power.

Fall down!
Deeper than you knew you could
    onto nothing solid—
    net-less, suspended
    over black water
At the absolute end
    of everything you've been
    till now.

Strip-mined—
That's how it feels
    sitting in the wound
    that's seared upon your face,

Looking out to the world
 with a bleak eye
 and an empty heart.
A wound that can last
 a lifetime
 or an hour.

Don't try to heal it too soon.
Let it gape out into the open air—
A gash upon your landscape
 that can be
 the opening to a new world
 that only wizards know.

And then only heart
 to heart
 to heart.

PART FOUR
RECEPTIVITY
Opening to Conversation

*If you are humble nothing will touch you,
neither praise nor disgrace,
because you know what you are.*

MOTHER TERESA

The Bridge at Maam

"This is where you get out," he said.
Not the cozy village you'd expected—
    with shops and neat streets,
    park benches, tea rooms,
    hanging baskets of bright flowers,
    familiar sights all scrubbed up
    for tourists.

For you, the end of the line comes
    at a narrow pull-off
    just past a crossroads
    you did not note as special.

With all your friends heading off
    to a mountain ramble,
    your destination is a singular pub
    back over a bridge
    you did not know you'd crossed—
    the final span
    marking a fulfillment,
    the point of no return
And a choice.

"Watch out for bachelor farmers,"
    they called after you.
"If they show you their watches
    and start numbering their acres,
    we may not see you again!"

It happened once, the story goes,
    when a lady traveler
    ran away with a charmer
    she met in such a place.

But you're not looking for romance.

Your choice is simpler:
    to sit in a corner
    and write gloomy verse
    or to speak out of your vulnerability
    and ask for directions.

Sometimes that's all it takes
    to restart the engine of life—
    a word of inquiry that
    honors hospitality.

And suddenly you're talking
    with new friends,
    sharing stories, a pint or two,
    and common observations.

Not realizing until later
    that the most humble of conversations
    has deposited in your heart
    a passport to hope,
    the end of life as you've known it,
    and the way to future possibility.

CHAPTER 8

An Invitation and a Choice

While on a walking tour in Ireland, I sprained my knee and couldn't go on the final hike, although I did get to travel with the group on a bus ride through some gorgeous country that included lunch in a charming village. The guide had kindly offered that they would drop me off at the local pub at Maam (pronounced "Mahm"), where I could spend a couple of hours until they picked me up after their walk.

I had visions of a village similar to the one where we had stopped for lunch. But after a half-hour's drive through increasingly wild territory, the van stopped abruptly and the guide said, "This is where you get out."

There was no sign of civilization except for some deserted boats tied to a small dock and a lone pub back across the bridge we had just crossed. I had no choice but to go where I was directed.

There were two doors: one marked Bar and one marked Lounge. I chose Lounge and took a seat in the

Part Four: Receptivity - Opening to Conversation

furthest corner—not knowing what to do. I pulled out my journal but had no desire to write down the gloomy thoughts that filled my mind.

There was no waitress, so I went up to the bar to order a drink—an action easier planned than executed. The lounge bar also connected to the other room and the bartender was all the way at the end where some "bachelor farmers" were drinking.

As I stood there looking confused, a lovely retired couple having their lunch and a pint offered their assistance. The husband elicited a drink order from me and called out to the bartender, "Mary, get the lady what she wants to drink, won't ye?"

I thanked him, took a sip of the beverage that Mary had quickly served, and made a decision to answer the Unknown's invitation. "Where are you from?" I asked.

With that single exchange, the couple and I became instant friends. We talked for the full three hours that the tour group was on its hike. And I learned a big lesson about choosing to receive a gift that was right in front of me.

A bit of desperate openness on my part reaped a bounty of hospitality from the locals. It seems a small event, but it was a turning point in my experience of what had been a physically and emotionally demanding journey.

Accepting the Invitation

After the brittle hardness of resistance, it is a relief to

An Invitation and a Choice

entertain the soft warmth of receptivity that conveys a natural hospitality. It invites us to consider change differently. Not as an enemy to be defeated, but as a generous host that offers opportunity for learning and growth.

Of course, if change is an invitation and receptivity a choice, then the future depends on how I choose:

- Will I continue to resist or will I engage?
- Can I receive the gift of possibility that arrives on my doorstep, even if it comes in a crumpled box with torn wrapping paper?
- Am I willing to trust the Unknown and enter into the deeply feminine mystery of the darkness?

I discovered that if I could receive what happened without resistance, I was on my way to transformation. Here is what my Wise Inner Counselor had to say:

Change is not going to immediately reveal its secrets. At this stage, nothing is figure-out-able; so don't try.

Do your best to accept that the lights have gone out and you don't have a torch. Admit that you're clueless and alone, probably more frightened than you have ever been.

Open your mind to the idea that you can learn to see in the dark. Relax, breathe, and consider that the Void is full of potential. Can you become the seed that goes into the ground to grow into a mighty green plant?

Understand that the moon has a dark side, and so do you. Not evil, but hidden. Full of potential, opportunity, and options. Are you willing to be taught? To see with subtle eyes? To accept this invitation to dance in the moonlight?

Encouraging Receptivity

At the beginning of a weekend retreat I facilitated on loss and grief, I asked the group about receptivity. I wanted to know why they had decided to attend when others who had inquired ultimately did not show up.

"What was it that encouraged you to travel here in spite of your fears?" I asked.

"You did," came the surprising answer.

The fact that I had answered their e-mails and the retreat center staff had taken their calls had made all the difference. Hearing a friendly voice on the other end of the line had helped them feel safe to venture into this particular corner of the Unknown.

When faced with a foreign situation, it really does help to have an encouraging guide, someone who has been where we are going. Every situation of dramatic change is unique, but we can be comforted in the knowledge that others have gone through similar circumstances.

These similarities lead me to believe that there is an inner geometry of change. The manner in which it manifests in each of our lives will be specific to our circumstance. Yet there is this moving stream, this flow that has a consistent wisdom to it that allows it to appear in whatever way is most appropriate.

An Invitation and a Choice

In its brilliance, what change does—and what helps create receptivity in us—is that it sets us in direct confrontation with a realization:

If I don't do something different, I'm going to feel this rotten forever. And I choose not to do that. I could do better. I <u>want</u> to do better, but I need help. I can't do this alone. This isn't the whole story. I need to write the next chapter of my life.

Change muscles us right up against those thoughts and feelings like a log across the stream. And part of the invitation of receptivity is to step over that log or push it out of the way by saying yes to what is arising. By saying yes to the flow.

Workshop participants often tell me that they felt an inner prompting to attend the event. It is not uncommon for them to say, "I just knew in my heart that this was the right thing for me to do."

So, to be receptive is to possess a heart that is willing to hear an inner call to embrace the Unknown and to act on it. The heart knows the way. And yet the question remains:

How can I create receptivity if I don't feel it? I may believe in a positive outcome from this change, but how do I get there when I'm feeling overwhelmed, angry, and confused?

The answer is inquiry. Receptivity is not passive acquiescence. It is a dynamic, intentional conversation between fact and feeling. Dealing with facts can help us relax from resistance and fear and de-escalate the volatile energies that swirl around a life-altering event.

Reducing this emotional charge can help us replace resistance with a spacious attitude that opens the door to possibility. By first asking *What happened?* and listing the facts, we are giving our emotions a break while we get on with the business of creating a framework for dealing with present circumstances.

It is biologically impossible to be hotly emotional and coolly analytical at the same time. Listing the facts of what happened is like releasing the valve on a pressure cooker. We lower the heat, reduce the friction, take the struggle out of coping, and turn it into processing. We stop wringing our hands and—like the farmer whose donkey was stuck in the well—we get busy shoveling.

In a calmer atmosphere, inquiry can begin to do its subtle work of detection. Once we have the facts, we are better mentally equipped to infer, imagine, connect, and collaborate on developing solutions that address rather than compound the initial chaos.

So receptivity becomes the ineluctable, inescapable determination that says:

Yes, I have a choice to resist or engage. And if I want to thrive in this situation, I have absolutely <u>no choice</u> but to engage. I <u>must</u> do this.

CHAPTER 9

Hospitality and the New Story

Question 1: How have I been prepared?
When change is upon you, ask yourself this question
to identify what you know, what you can do, and
who you are as an individual.

Receptivity encourages us to accept the reality of our situation. To recognize our ability to deal with those facts. To begin the conversation through which a new narrative can unfold along the journey that is actually a series of three stories.

Story One is about the past—a tale so familiar we don't even realize it's the first thing we hear upon waking. Rehearsed and polished over many years, Story One is what we tell the world and ourselves about who we are: age, gender, marital status, number of children, sexual preference, hobbies, education, employment history, title, and so forth.

Part Four: Receptivity - Opening to Conversation

We may also include a few defining characteristics such as generous, kind, hardworking, or shrewd. It's a sort of mental job description we fill out each morning—a useful shorthand for how we structure our lives and for how others see us at the most superficial levels.

To be perfectly honest, this summary may be all we need for much of our daily business. But there is a lot more to us than name, title, and social security number. Just below the job description lies a complex array of opinions and value judgments about where we fit into the world as we know it.

It can be a poignant experience to be in the company of anyone who has entered the thin place of transition between one phase of life and another. The elderly or the dying are particularly drawn to conducting a personal life inventory in which they review their past thoughts, deeds, and actions.[8] Assessing their place in a world they helped to create, they ask themselves: *What legacy am I leaving behind? Was I a good person? Did my life have meaning?*

These are fundamental questions we would all do well to ask before things change—because life is so much more than a data sheet. That's one reason why flux can be so hard. We don't just replace key information with a simple update. When the tale we tell about who we are no longer applies, we are shaken to the foundation of being.

Story Two—the unsettling account of what is now so dramatically different—affects the whole tapestry of life, because it challenges our beliefs about what is true. It can feel like a horror story, a nightmare that unwelcome change has plopped us into.

And it is so confusing. *If everything I once believed has changed, then what was the first story all about?*

Our sense-making framework has been seriously disrupted and we don't understand it. We want to know who or what is to blame.

As if we could send back to an errant universe the earthquake that has turned our tidy world into chaos, we ask: *Why? Why me? Why not somebody who deserves to be punished? Why now?*

When change is sudden, unexpected, and still fresh, we might ask, *How have I been prepared for this?* But our most natural response is likely to be, *I haven't been. I never thought such a thing could happen to me.*

We don't know where to begin writing the future's narrative, because Story Three must emerge from a mystery we are only beginning to perceive. Optimists among us predict a happy ending—and we would, oh, so love to believe them. But past failures and our natural tendency to doubt what we cannot see have already woven threads of mistrust into our thinking.

When the world feels like so much quicksand, we need something solid to work from. Identifying our talents provides that platform. We can build it by asking some personal questions:

Part Four: Receptivity - Opening to Conversation

- What knowledge, skills, and competencies come naturally to me—especially when there is a challenge at hand?
- What particular talents always seem to emerge from me, regardless of what I'm doing or where I'm doing it?
- If I were a jug of fresh, unpasteurized milk straight from the cow, what is the cream that would rise to the top?

If our paying job does not make direct use of our talents, these innate abilities may provide a running theme for how we approach our work. And they may be so natural that we don't even recognize them as strengths. For example:

- Do I immediately drill down to the bottom line of a situation, pulling out the essential facts or the numbers and costs?
- Am I the one who starts organizing the details, bringing order to chaos, creating a priority list and a timeline?
- Do I have a gift with people that allows me to mediate differences, soften rough edges, and pull together a team?
- Am I the idea person, the one who thinks outside the box to create innovative solutions? [9]

Nestled inside of talent is what I like to call our *core virtue*. In other words, if we were to suddenly disappear, what gift of our presence would be missing for those who depend on us?

Like Jimmy Stewart's character in the classic movie *It's a Wonderful Life*, most people can't identify their core virtue. At best, they will fall back on what they do, but that's not who they are. They need somebody else to point it out to them.

To discover our own core virtue, we may have to ask those who have known and appreciated us for years. And we may be surprised at how quickly they can articulate what makes us most irreplaceable to them.

Irene's Story

Irene was stuck with a truly horrible boss. At the time, she was much less assertive than she is today, and he took advantage of her reticence.

To help her overcome her understandable feeling of vulnerability, I suggested that she ask her two adult sons what they most admired about her as their mother and as a person. Independently and without hesitation, they each replied, "You are the strongest person I have ever known."

Hearing that unequivocal declaration was the beginning of Irene's turnaround. Over the next several weeks, she reclaimed her innate strength and began the process of extricating herself from a toxic environment.

Irene is also an enormously kind person, and she naturally exercised her renewed confidence with grace. It wasn't so much what she said or did; it was that she now consciously radiated strength, dignity, and self-respect. Each successful interaction with her boss encouraged her for the next confrontation.

Not surprisingly, her confidence prompted others to speak up. The nasty boss was soon let go and Irene was promoted to a better position in the company.

Initiating the New Story

Like Irene, when we're in a crisis we need to know how and where we add value. It is this unique combination of knowledge, skills, competencies, talent, and heart that has not only prepared us to meet the difficulties of change, it has in fact made us the best possible person to take on a challenge that might defeat someone else.

When we can acknowledge our ability to respond, we initiate Story Three—the new story of our life as an overcomer. Now receptive to the strength of our own core virtue, we cease to be a victim. This self-respect engenders balanced power that others notice.

We may initiate the rising tide that raises everyone else's boat. We begin to see our way through the Middle of Nowhere even as we become a beacon for those whom we may unknowingly inspire.

Rekindling self-respect is not the whole story. There is another level to core virtue. When Irene described how she had put her strength into action, I asked what made her receptive to the idea that indeed she was strong.

"It was love," she said. "My sons and I share an abiding mutual respect. I knew they were telling me the truth about myself. I could not dishonor them by rejecting it—I love them too much for that. So I summoned that love, pulled myself together, and started acting like the strong woman they know. That's when everything began to improve."

What Irene demonstrated in her own Middle of Nowhere was how to transform *Why me?* into *Why not me?* She was not the only employee being tormented by her boss, but she was the first one to take a stand.

With some coaching, she assessed the facts of her situation, including her previously established reputation as a valued employee. She recognized her core virtue. And in putting that strength to work, she became receptive to the deeper question at the heart of Question 1: *How am I expressing love in this situation?*

Whether it is through courage, kindness, humor, clarity of mind, creativity, generosity, or perseverance, the moment we make contact with that essence of love in our own hearts, we have begun the hospitable conversation with change. Everything starts to shift, and the new narrative of Story Three will be the outcome.

Part Four: Receptivity - Opening to Conversation

The conclusion of *How have I been prepared?* is that we do not allow difficult circumstances, our own doubt, or other people's attitudes to define us in terms of weakness. We identify with that part of us that is honest, powerful, and imbued with love—knowing that love is the source of our preparation for the conversation with change.

A new level of self-discovery emerges from that realization, enhancing our use of affirmation. As we move through each subsequent question in The LIGHT Process, our affirmations grow deeper in meaning and richer in their ability to inspire us.

Each spiral of inquiry prompts expanded affirmative responses that include and then transcend what came before. So here in the Middle of Nowhere we affirm our strength and our ability to continue the journey with courage and a more powerful sense of self than we had at the beginning of our experience with change.

Affirmation 1
Life has prepared me for my current situation.
My core virtue was always there;
I just needed a reminder.

Mind the Thresholds

Life is precarious at transition points
    where the soul steps out
        once again into uncharted waters.

Flush with accomplishment
    she may be reckless—
    a bit too sure of future success
    even greedy for what comes next.

Mind the gap, as they say;
    fortunes can slip from our grasp
    in the split second
    between here and there.

For there is always an interval—
    the in-breath e're action is taken
    a moment of decision:
        What to do
        and how to be
        in the doing.

At the cliff edge—
    in the mist of expectation
    and the gathering storm
    of possibility
    nothing is clear.

Life begins anew each time
>   a turning point is reached
>   for past is always prologue
>   and genius never guaranteed.

Mind the thresholds
>   so your transformation
>   may be complete
>   the butterfly fully formed
>   and the hands of your clock
>   ticking happy hours
>   for cycles without ending.

Many fear the razor's edge—
>   the ineluctable choice
>   to take what seems
>   a perilous chance.

But saying *Yes!* to the Unknown
>   can bring life's
>   greatest blessings.

What will you say, my dear?

PART FIVE
RECONNECTION
Waking Up and Showing Up

*I am part of you, and I am within you.
Seek me within and without,
and you will be strong.*

*Know me.
Venture into the dark
so that you may awaken to
Balance, Illumination, and Wholeness.*

*Take my Love with you everywhere
and find the Power within
to be who you wish.*

Unknown

One Hopes...

To be guided
    by the walk itself
To be walked
    by the path
To be spirited
    by the air
    and the sea
    and the mist
    that shrouds you
    from the others
So that each
    may walk alone
    surrounded
    by the true companions
    of one's heart:
The loved
    the lost
    the not yet found
    and most of all
    the presence of
    the One that touches
    all that is.

CHAPTER 10

Waking Up to Inner Truth

To reconnect is to wake up. Engage. Plug in. Look around and feel. Come out of the numbness that may have clouded our minds in the early days of volatility.

In the flow of reconnection, we notice the call and response of a deeply personal dialogue. Transition invites us to action and we respond. We summon our inner strengths and they show up. Like waves upon the shore, we move in a relational dance of question and answer—back and forth, in and out between the tension of uncertainty and the calm of insight.

As with many aspects of change, reconnection is a paradox. It is active and vibrant while also being observant. There is a stillness to it that encourages us to follow the thread of self-appreciation into a deep meditation on the source of our special talents and gifts.

In the midst of tackling real-world situations that require reinvention, the conversation that naturally began in receptivity moves into relationship with an element of consciousness that facilitates communication between the Unseen and the seen.

Nearly every conceptual system has coined a term for this inner guide. Some focus on an inherent divinity of the *still, small voice*. Others refer to *conscience*, the inner voice of reason that points out moral dilemmas. Still others prefer *intuition*, the ability to gain direct knowledge independent of mental reasoning.

I call it the *True Self* or the *Wise Inner Counselor*—the inner voice of authenticity that speaks directly into the human heart on behalf of the Divine.

Rather than merely hearing an occasional whisper from our True Self, in reconnection we intentionally focus our awareness upon listening for its guidance. For most of us, the road to that awakening involves some kind of centering practice.

The discipline we choose is a highly personal decision and not something anyone can prescribe for another. So, before considering *what* constitutes any stabilizing activity, I decided to look behind the *how* of practice into the *why* that motivates it.

If the purpose of receptivity is recognition of our core virtue, then reconnection can be seen as intentional bonding with the Wise Inner Counselor.

Part Five: Reconnection - Waking Up and Showing Up

Any relationship takes daily practice. This one also requires courage to overcome the negative feedback that many of us have received merely for following the inner voice's encouragement to express our true nature.

We inhabit a world threatened by authenticity, even as it craves it. Early in life, our natural inclinations may have rendered us so radically different from those around us that we have learned to keep these precious gifts safely under wraps.

In too many cases, our unique talents have been the most maligned, ignored, hidden, or stifled aspects of our being. We even may have forgotten that we have talents—except that there is something so indomitable about the human spirit. Those special qualities do have a way of shining through. Our present task is to wake up and consciously put them into action.

Dramatic change cracks us wide open, shatters our facades, and pulls down the fortresses we have erected around our gifts. In those moments when life as we have known it is irreparably altered, the only reliable truth is that essence of authenticity that has been our internal beacon—despite the world's relentless attempts to ignore or snuff it out.

This stage of The LIGHT Process is dedicated to reconnecting with that real, authentic Self.

CHAPTER 11

Creating Emotional Congruence

In the early phases of life-altering shake-ups, *trust no one* is often a wise course of action until we can assess how individuals—ourselves included—are dealing with the upset.

When crisis first erupts, many of us may become unbalanced, operating from a chaotic and disconnected state of mind. Ordinarily this is a temporary condition and, as the situation stabilizes, we find our way back to a more centered response that is known as *emotional congruence*.

Unfortunately, rather than rallying their inner resources to deal with the disruption and move on, some people remain unbalanced beyond the initial stage of a crisis. One challenge we face when we interact with these people is that their outer appearance and behavior may not match their inner feelings.

Emotionally congruent people smile when they are happy. Incongruent persons may smile widest when they are sad or anxious—or worse, when they are angry.

Part Five: Reconnection - Waking Up and Showing Up

Inevitably, we bump up against their inconsistent behaviors and lack of emotional integration. If we stick around long enough, we may uncover the sad fact that the falsehoods they tell us reflect the lies they tell themselves.

Even more difficult is the discovery that, at times, we ourselves can also be masters of fabrication. Until we become aware of it, we can't help ourselves; it's how many of us have been raised. From earliest childhood we may have learned that our heartfelt desires are not appreciated by those in authority over us.

I know of several adults whose response to a young person's request to try something new and exciting is, "Oh, you wouldn't want to do that, would you?"

"Gee, I guess not," is the child's predictable and well-schooled answer. The matter is not raised again.

So whatever the desire, it is disowned and firmly repressed. We may feel like stuffed animals—crammed full of the dissociated ideas, hopes, dreams, innovations, and creative ways of self-expression that somebody convinced us were not welcome. These precious aspects of our being reflect an inner reality we have not dared voice or even admit to ourselves.

Regaining access to those long-stifled truths comprises some of the deepest work of the self-realization journey. Unfortunately, even spiritual practices do not necessarily bring us to an awareness of what is really going on in our psyche. For that exercise, we may find it helpful

Creating Emotional Congruence

to turn to the animal kingdom, to one of mankind's most ancient companions: the horse.

People who deceive themselves about what they are thinking and feeling can have a lot of trouble with horses. In her profound book *The Tao of Equus*, author Linda Kohanov describes the origin of this behavior:

> The common human habit of suppressing negative or socially unacceptable feelings is notoriously unsettling to a species that survives by being able to gauge a predator's presence and intentions at a distance. A person who is "emotionally incongruent," who acts one way while feeling the opposite, appears dangerously out of focus to the equine awareness system.[10]

Kohanov goes on to describe how her most sensitive therapy horse will shy away from a client who is putting on a brave or happy face to mask feelings of fear or sadness. Conversely, when the same person verbalizes those feelings, the mare calms down and allows herself to be groomed—even if the client is still fearful or sad.

The key here is that honest expression of inner emotions causes body language to become congruent with feelings, even if they are negative. Horses don't judge human emotion as right or wrong. To them it is merely information that determines whether or not they feel safe with what is going on around them.

What horses do so masterfully register is the correlation between a human's emotional energy and her body language. If they don't match, the horse is unsettled and outpictures in her own behavior the attitudes of which the human may be shockingly unaware.

Centering Practice: A Horse Story

About a year ago I decided that something was missing from my own centering practice, which sampled several modalities but focused on none. I did some yoga and Pilates, a bit of T'ai Chi, plus daily meditation, affirmative prayers, and chants designed to invoke spiritual energy into personal and global concerns.

Each provided a unique contribution to my path of self-actualization, but none was sufficiently satisfying for me to claim it as my preferred practice. So in my early sixties, I decided to explore the world of horseback riding and equine therapy.

At one of my first riding lessons, I had occasion to test Kohanov's theory of emotional congruence. Had I not already considered the value of telling your horse the truth, I would have canceled my riding lesson for the day.

I was feeling annoyed and out of sorts because of a persistently troubling family situation. I knew I should let the conversation's negativity roll off, but nothing I tried

Creating Emotional Congruence

seemed to dispel the toxic emotions I had absorbed. I was genuinely afraid of bringing that energy into the arena—lest the horse mirror it back to me.

As many riders and therapists will tell you, merely coming into contact with horse energy can be calming. During a pre-lesson conversation with my instructor, I almost forgot my grumpiness. Then, on the way to catch and groom RC, the gelding I normally rode, I remembered: *Tell the horse the truth.* So I did.

"RC, I'm having a tough day," I said as I patted the black bay on his left shoulder and gently stroked his long back. "I almost didn't come today, but I knew you would understand."

And you know what—I think he did. Perhaps it was my imagination, or the fact that I took extra time grooming the horse, reminding myself to slow down and really focus on his silky coat and supple body. Whatever the reason, RC seemed especially affectionate and accepting of me that day. He even let me use a soft brush to clean some dirt from his face.

By the time the grooming session was complete, I was calm and ready to ride. Because my energy was centered, the lesson was a pleasant one for me and apparently for the horse. Later that afternoon, the thought came to me:

Imagine if your practice connected you with a being that is incapable of falsehood. How would you carry that energy into your daily life—especially into your response to change?

Part Five: Reconnection - Waking Up and Showing Up

Remember the feeling of emotional congruence you experienced today when you told your horse the truth. That is what happens in conversation with your impeccable Wise Inner Counselor. Follow this sensation to develop personal integrity.

The purpose of practice is to learn to tell the truth.

CHAPTER 12

From Coping to Processing

Some days it feels as if the world is blowing apart. When we see entire communities decimated by Nature's fury or innocent bystanders terrorized by acts of human cruelty, we can only wonder how to navigate so much upheaval.

The ferocious velocity of change taking place in the world must surely prompt each of us to consider what we would do in a crisis. Of course, dealing with life-altering events is a concept most of us do not care to entertain. Perhaps we are even a bit superstitious that imagining our lives being upended will invite disaster.

Despite our reticence, we have seen that the absence of a plan can make a terrible situation worse, while the presence of those trained as first responders can greatly reduce the life-threatening consequences of a sudden and destructive event.

In other words, in case of emergency, we need a life raft. Knowing our strengths and having practiced in

Part Five: Reconnection - Waking Up and Showing Up

advance how to apply them can provide such an effective safety measure.

I remember watching an interview with a retired U. S. Army sergeant after a giant tornado had wiped out the Oklahoma City suburb where he lived. Having served multiple tours of duty in Iraq and Afghanistan, he went right to work helping search-and-rescue efforts at the elementary school across the street from where his own house had been damaged. As I recall, here is what he said:

"It's what I do," he stated matter-of-factly to the television interviewer who stood in amazement at his composure. "Of course, this kind of destruction never really sinks in until it's your own home," he said, ruefully looking around at an entire neighborhood of twisted trees and rubble.

"I know how to help people in these situations," he continued. "I'll be okay, but I'm not sure they will."

What I understood him to mean was that his well-practiced ability to take meaningful action in the face of overwhelming chaos was extremely useful in the aftermath of widespread destruction. It was also his personal life raft that he would use to transform coping strategies into personal growth.

The use of inquiry is another important aspect of being prepared. Here are some questions we might want to pose in advance of inevitable future change—to develop a habit of self-examination before we really need it.

- When the earth quakes, which self shows up when I do?
- Is my first responder a loving, courageous True Self that can improve difficult situations?
- Or does a fearful, false self begin maneuvering to its own advantage?

Experienced first responders know that effectively handling chaos is not a test we can cram for, which is why they practice lifesaving procedures until those techniques become instant reflexes. For the rest of us, learning to deal with seemingly insignificant adjustments can prepare us for the big ones.

In the early days of overwhelming calamity, it is enough to cope, to take one step and then another, to do whatever is in front of us. This is a time to reach out to our fellow creatures, respond in love, and keep breathing.

However, coping alone is not sufficient. The phrase *to cope* actually means to maintain a contest or combat with something. Thus, even the most skillful coping strategies remain a form of resistance. As long as we are unwilling or unable to engage the full reality of change, we cannot truly learn or grow from it.

That is why we emphasize *process* as a natural and organic, inside-out phenomenon of gradual adjustment.

Part Five: Reconnection - Waking Up and Showing Up

In other words, to effectively deal with change, we must allow ourselves to be moved and transformed by it.

Learning to mentally and emotionally integrate the mind-numbing shock of sudden disruption and then grow amidst the countless challenges that follow is what dramatic change calls us to do. We must hold strong to our personal life raft, engaging our distinctive oars of internal and external strength as we row with new confidence to what can seem like a far-distant shore.

If we cower on the sands of the past, we may miss the blessing of future insight. If we timidly wade in the shallows, sooner or later a big wave is going to knock us down. The only way over to safety is through the emotional water. The only way through is to venture into the depths of uncertainty.

We must face the Unknown and learn its ways if we are to make it all the way through to the fresh start that awaits us on the other side of nowhere.

CHAPTER 13

Showing Up for Authenticity

Question 2: How am I staying afloat?
Many people find that a regular practice such as meditation, centering prayer, or physical exercise helps them weather the storms of dramatic change.

This stage of the journey requires great courage, because we are sailing rough waters in faith. We hope there will be a light at the end of the voyage, but right now we're still in the dark. We have made progress, but we remain awash in unpredictable currents.

All too often we get this far and then decide to quit. We are not even midway into the process and yet we are ready to return to a familiar harbor. In our minds we may rail against a world that has visited chaos upon us:

Okay, I'm done now. I've been really brave. I've been strong. I've proved I can cope. See, I've done it! Game over. Make it all go away now.

Part Five: Reconnection - Waking Up and Showing Up

We vacillate. We hesitate. Ideally, we will eventually ease back on course, take a deep breath, and courageously persevere. But bouts of indecision are normal.

In this deeply foreign place, we are so much more aware of separation than we are of connection. Although we have gained new awareness of our talents and may be experiencing greater integration with our feelings as well as with our Wise Inner Counselor, this phase of the change journey can be daunting.

So much more is unknown than is known. A literal twist of fate has flipped our reality. What was once a tidy circle of life has been disconnected and reattached with a bend in the middle.

We can still imagine what used to be. We long for it, but we can't touch it. We may even catch a glimpse of the future that we call the *Beautiful Middle of Now Here*. Unfortunately, there are yet miles to cover before we will reach that promised land. For now, we are neither here nor there, and a veil of mystery lies between.

We can recall the past and postulate a future, but we can't reach either. We can't make the connection happen. We can't force it or grasp it. The only way to cross over is to relax, sit with the feeling of disconnection, and discover the passage that lies within separation itself.

Practicing emotional congruence fosters personal integrity and loyalty to our True Self. Impeccability is the way through the veil, across the divide that separates both past and future from the present. It creates in us the hospitable heart that secures our invitation to cross over to the other side of change.

Invitation to the Dance

Uncertainty on any scale can destroy not only our physical moorings but our internal ones as well. When our practice dispels doubt and worthlessness, it is a useful one. When it fosters emotional congruity and an ability to discern deep inner truth, it is an activity to be encouraged.

Skillful practice is re-creational, not mere avoidance of problems or the deeper work of self-actualization. With calm, engaged attention, effective practice has a quality of rejuvenation about it that facilitates our communion in that soul space where earthly time evaporates.

This is the habitation of the Wise Inner Counselor, where we can lose the sense of separation, finding instead a profound connection with all of life. It is that juicy place of ideation where innovations and solutions come sailing into our awareness, almost as if by magic.

There is a limitless feeling to this plane of consciousness where the line blurs between the concrete and the imaginative. Many people equate it with spirituality. But whatever we call it, entering into this thin place can propel us into a spacious forward movement that is exactly what we need to gain momentum in our journey through and eventually out of the Middle of Nowhere.

Part Five: Reconnection ~ Waking Up and Showing Up

In this realm of reconnection, we discover new aspects of our True Self. Fear and doubt have no place here because they don't flow. They restrict growth and bind us to the past, whereas reconnection is all about the freedom and acceptance of the present moment.

Here we feel creative, capable of new thought and insight. We may develop a sense of partnership with something larger than our human self. And as we practice this collaboration, it can morph from an occasional heightened state of awareness into a daily way of showing up for life.

Of course, any practice can become a trap. If we slide into rote repetition, we are in danger of becoming victims of our own dogma. If habit devolves into a chain forged in the iron of fear, we may end up bound to the past, rigid in our beliefs, and resistant to—or incapable of—receiving new inspiration for our journey through change.

However, when our practice connects us in flexible conversation with the unseen world of the imagination, we will more likely continue to grow in authenticity and personal power. So, what and how each of us practices can be evaluated with the question *How does my practice move me forward?*

If at any point we begin to feel that we have painted ourselves into a perceptual corner, we can reevaluate our practice to detect where it no longer serves our mission, our work, or our engagement with the True Self who so consistently shows up when we're really in the flow.

Practice is an invitation to the divine dance that lives at the heart of all creation. It is this interplay that navigates the Unknown, eliciting from it inspired prospects and practical, creative solutions.

So our next affirmation conveys a process of integration with our highest intentions. It intimates the divine cooperation that accomplishes infinitely more than fearfully bobbing along atop the ocean of change.

With practice, we can learn to engage the upsurges. To surf and glide not only upon, but also within the curls of the biggest waves.

Affirmation 2
*I practice daily being true to my Self,
who lives impeccably in the truth.*

Brushing the Horse's Tail

I am not the first to have stood here
    leaning ever so slightly
    against the sleek warm side
    of the big dark horse
    whose tail I'm brushing.

Many have gone before me
    to rest here in a moment
    out of time.

I see them standing in antiquity,
    combing out snarls
    in the long black hair,
    slowing down and sighing
    in a soft breeze
    that offers fresh perspective.

An hour is nothing in horse time.

Communion is all that matters,
    relaxing mental tangles,
    brushing the horse's tail.

PART SIX
RESONANCE
A Port in the Storm

While with an eye made quiet by the power
Of harmony, and the deep power of joy,
We see into the life of things.

WILLIAM WORDSWORTH

Sean-nós

Be silent, still
>until you feel the breath take you—
filling, emptying,
moving the reed to tune,
touching a secret place
that only the full heart knows.

The flame sparks,
>bursting with a bonfire's light
that contains all,
expresses all,
consumes all,
and will not be denied.

Be that fire
>in sound and step,
in joyful noise,
as David's harp did play
and as he sang and danced
in jubilant exultation.

CHAPTER 14

Getting in Sync

Like a cosmic transporter, beautiful music can take me apart and put me back together in an entirely different state of mind. When I experience a powerful symphony, such as Beethoven's *Ninth* or Mahler's *Sixth*, I am translated out of normal, everyday awareness.

Change effects a similar result as it un-moors us from our previous way of being. Once unleashed, even planned conversions can shake us to the core, causing us to move in unforeseen directions and behave in ways we never expected.

This sense of being lifted out of ourselves offers keen insight into how to navigate transition's foreign territory: by paying attention to what is arising in the moment, deeply experiencing our emotions, taking in every physical sensation, and following that information's guidance.

When we allow ourselves to be moved in this way, we may discover that we have become co-creators with

Getting in Sync

change. We have become participants in the divine dance of transformation.

On my second trip to Ireland, I had occasion to hear a type of music that does just that. *Sean-nós* is a form of highly ornamented traditional Irish singing that not only transports the solo singer and listeners to other worlds, it seems to descend from elsewhere with an innate intelligence that acts according to its own inner logic.

That is certainly what I felt when I heard the world-renowned sean-nós singer Nóirín Ní Ríain[11] perform in her native land. Her a cappella songs are absolutely stunning in their ability to move her audience.

Even the ancient tunes in her repertoire have an extemporaneous quality, and her mellifluous ornamentation feels improvisational. The sound she produces seems effortless. After hearing her several times, I realized the secret: *She's not singing, she's being sung.*

I believe this is what happens with anyone great—be they artists, teachers, musicians, inventors, dancers, salespeople, painters, welders, sculptors, or surgeons. They study for years, learning their craft and learning it well. And then, at a certain point, they put away the technique and simply perform on the stage of their profession. Like Nóirín, they allow themselves to be sung.

Nóirín seems very relaxed in person—as if she has conquered all sense of doubt in her creative process. It seems that she has so merged with her music that the

Part Six: Resonance - A Port in the Storm

Divine Musician, who has always been her inspiration, participates in her performance. Listening to her sing was like witnessing a vocal *pas de deux* that floated between worlds.

Perhaps she has so often experienced the presence of celestial partners that she now trusts them to show up at the right time. Music critics say she has the voice of an angel. It could be that angels sing through her because she offers no resistance to their presence.

The Cosmic Homing Device

Achieving this level of spontaneity is what it means to resonate with the truth that we focus on in our centering practice. Reconnection flows directly into resonance, and it is in this harmonious relationship of co-creation that we begin to understand what it means to live on the razor's edge of change.

Practice teaches us to tell the truth and to discern it when we hear it. We learn to recognize the cosmic homing device of the Wise Inner Counselor's vibration, to value it above all negative voices of self-criticism and doubt, and to follow its intimations when they slip through to our outer awareness.

Silence is essential. If we can quiet the chattering mind and learn to perceive and connect with truth in practice, then illumination follows through resonance. These are the moments of greatest inspiration and true collaboration between the Unseen and the seen.

Getting in Sync

We are nearly out of the wilderness. Doubt dissolves into confidence and worry melts into joy as we recognize the power for good that we can generate when we consciously work as co-creators with the Unseen. With help so readily available, our arduous journey through change takes on a new flavor of optimism.

The key to this work is to maintain an open, compassionate heart and an awareness that is grounded in a body that acts as a barometer to measure the intensity of present circumstances.

A grounded body also functions as a cosmic radio that receives information from the Wise Inner Counselor and then broadcasts it to our conscious awareness in the form of physical sensations. With focused repetition, we can learn to read these sensations as clearly as the words on this page.

CHAPTER 15

Listening to the Body

The body never lies. But like Cassandra's prophecies about the Trojan War, which were ignored,[13] its warnings often go unheeded until illness or calamity strikes.

Many centering practices take us out of the body into the egoless realm of pure mind and heart. This is the essence of spiritual discipline that cultivates deep communion in a state of universal oneness designed to lift our desires out of fearful grasping into loving generosity.

Especially in today's frantic world, it is both useful and psychologically healthy to step out of the maelstrom with a daily meditative practice. But because most of us are called to take action in the midst of change, we cannot abide forever in retreat. We must also engage in the physical plane.

A couple of questions arise from this challenge:
- What activity requires full participation of all our senses while also triggering our intuition?

- What endeavor requires our highest level of attention, integrity, impeccability, agility, and strength while achieving creative flow?

Fortunate are those whose work offers such inspired freedom. For many of us, a hobby or avocation is more likely the source. And some have cultivated a daily practice that accomplishes both grounding and elevation.

Our goal is to find an activity that encourages all of the senses to resonate together so that we are operating in a kind of *fluid present* that incorporates the recent past as well as the near future. Here we are fully engaged in the moment. We are keenly aware of the body's subtle messages. We also have a sense of what's next—and of what action or inaction is necessary to get there.

Musicians who are accomplished sight-readers do this naturally. So do actors in their initial read-through of a script. When approaching a piece of music or literature for the first time, those who are skilled in their craft read a little bit ahead even as they give each note or word its due. In that flow they feel what's coming, because the future makes itself known in that tiny space of rest that happens just before the in-breath.

Likewise, it is during inhalation that we set our intention for what manifests on the exhalation. When we are relaxed, our breath flows naturally and our belly is soft. In this receptive state, deep somatic insight more easily reaches our awareness, coming through the *chi* point below the navel, identified by martial artists as the body's life force center.[14]

Conversely, when we are tense we constrict our breathing and tighten our belly, setting up an energetic impediment to the flow of *chi* and our body's wisdom.

This is one reason that so many centering practices emphasize following the breath. Over time deep breathing opens pathways to higher consciousness, throwing wide the gate to heightened awareness.[15]

Of course, when we are open to the body's communication, we may not like what we hear—especially if the prevailing message is to slow down or not go ahead with something we are committed to. However, consistently following inner guidance enhances our ability to wisely apply the truth that a grounded body conveys.

Another Horse Story

They call him Tango—an apt name, as he seems to dance between the fragmented world of humans and the integrated one of his own equine species. Sometimes he shows a bit of attitude, yet he is an affectionate creature who elicits deep emotional response from his riders.

Ladies who attend his owner's retreats on basic and advanced equestrian skills often weep when they have to part with Tango. Having once experienced the power of connection untainted by human expectations or psychological projections, perhaps they doubt the probability of feeling it in their lives back home.

"Tango gets me," said one lady with a wistful tone that conveyed earnest feeling. I have come to understand what she meant.

I didn't fully appreciate Tango's special gift until I interacted with him. Watching others ride him didn't do it. I had to touch him, enter into his enormous energetic forcefield, and engage in the relationship of grooming and riding him.

"He's checking you out for treats," commented one of the other riders on the first day I was to work with Tango. He was snuffling around at my hands and hair and jeans pockets, allowing me to scratch him under his chin. I don't carry treats when I ride, so I doubt this was Tango's intention. My sense is that he was letting me know he was both physically and emotionally available.

"He loves to be groomed," called out his owner across the corral from where she was bridling another horse for the upcoming trail ride.

And I could feel it. The longer I handled Tango's body, brushing and combing his coat, scratching the itchy spots he can't reach, the deeper became our connection.

Once I was in the saddle and out on the trail, I felt his movements schooling mine, teaching me to loosen my hips and sway upon his back as we rode across a lush, open field. The feeling was invigorating.

Part Six: Resonance - A Port in the Storm

Things happen out on the trail as a horse navigates obstacles and adjusts to irregularities in the landscape, so I had to remain alert in order to shift with my mount. We were following another horse and experienced rider, but I was responsible for my interaction with Tango.

I had to pay close attention to my body and to his, without tensing up or mentally trying to do everything right. I couldn't space out or become distracted by the playful Black Angus calves that romped up to the fence to check us out.

Nor could I give in to Tango's tricks. Even at twenty-plus years old, he is a lively boy. And like most trail horses, he is eager to return to the safety of his corral after a ride.

"Don't let him take off on his own," warned my instructor. "You can ask him to trot, but he doesn't get to initiate it."

After an hour on Tango's back, I was feeling comfortable. So I asked him to walk, then to trot, then to slow again to a nice, easy walk. And then it happened. Almost without realizing it, I felt him *think* about trotting. I sensed the tiniest beginning of him gathering his energy to pick up the pace—and I perceived it before he could do it. Suddenly I understood what it meant to intuitively know something in the fluid present.

"Whoa, Tango," I said firmly, while gently pulling back on the reins. "I didn't ask for a trot, so you don't get to hurry."

We soon returned to the horse camp, where I unsaddled Tango, brushed him down, and gave him one last hug for the day. Leading him back to his corral, I realized:

This experience in the fluid present is how the Wise Inner Counselor cues us about where and how to be—and about who or what to avoid. The near future is contained in this moment that has emerged from the recent past. In the fluid present, they are all one.

Inner guidance comes sailing in to our outer awareness when we are gently focused in relaxed attention. In this receptive and engaged state, our bodies are grounded in their environment while our minds and hearts are attuned to finer vibrations.

Now we are able to function from that profound point between worlds where seen and Unseen meet to dance in perfect balance. This is the razor's edge.

Sensing

Feet touch earth
      on ancient stones
      cool, hard, rippled.

Water sings,
      splashing
      in the fountain.

Wind wraps the circle
      in its rushing,
      bending trees,
      clearing sky
      of clouds
      that disappear
      over grasslands
      in the distance.

Hands on carpet—
      soft, wooly,
      gentle comfort
      in a hard world.

How many senses
      would you
      be without?

Use them all
    and learn
        to read my wisdom.

Taste the present moment.

Breathe in the scent of harmony
    and know
    the heartbeat
    of the earth
    that folds you
    in her garments—
    if you will.

CHAPTER 16

Between the Unseen and the Seen

Driving across the barren landscape of Wyoming, I was reminded of the dangers along this road. Especially in winter and spring, sudden gusts of wind and snow can blow the unsuspecting traveler off the highway or into the path of oncoming traffic.

Such are the perils of the journey through change. Even when we make our way with receptive intention, new diversions are always possible. But having come so far, we must not fear to carry on. At this point in the Middle of Nowhere, a light is beginning to glimmer up ahead.

I could never understand why my late husband loved this stretch of road that I found boring. His fondness for its plainness escaped me until I began driving it alone.

Then, as with so many insights gained since his passing, I understood. In the stillness of empty highway, the landscape began to speak. Not in words or sounds, but in the language of sheer presence.

Suddenly, the connection of grasslands flowing into mountains rising up to meet an enormous sky where hawks and eagles soar impressed itself upon me. I began to comprehend what Wordsworth had meant when he wrote, "We see into the life of things." [16]

The interrelatedness of all life became profoundly clear as I felt myself enter a sense of timeless eternity, a space between worlds where the mundane becomes the miraculous and the All-in-all makes itself known.

Here is another facet of the razor's edge, I mused while maneuvering inclines and curves that cut across the otherwise trackless expanse. Far from being spaced out, my awareness was heightened by a certain luminosity that permeated the unfettered view. Largely untouched, the landscape exuded a powerful harmony and a joyful stillness that I had never before experienced.

All too quickly, I reached the outskirts of the next town. Immediately, a wave of sadness swept over me as I grieved for the mountaintop experience left behind. The sight of motels, gas stations, and other garish necessities of modern life assaulted my senses, which had only moments before so blissfully tasted the joy of living in a relational universe.

And still, as with a near-death experience, having once glimpsed that space between worlds, I knew I would never be the same. As I checked into a hotel for the night, I wondered:

Part Six: Resonance - A Port in the Storm

If a quiet eye and an open heart can result in such deep communion with the essence of life itself, is it possible to re-create the experience?

Can such a heightened state of awareness eventually become a familiar habitation? Is it possible to abide on the razor's edge between the Unseen and the seen, where time and space collapse and all is perfectly present?

For most of us, the answer to those questions is both no and yes. No—because eventually somebody has to cook dinner, wash the dishes, and take out the trash. As long as we live in physical form, the body will have needs that must be tended. And yes—because, having once stepped through the thin place between worlds, we will always carry a token of that awareness.

So we answer yes to the razor's edge—where change is ever present, where we discover that when we are mindful of the Wise Inner Counselor, even the most mundane tasks can be infused with its gentle guidance.

CHAPTER 17

Into the Fluid Present

Question 3: What do I need right now?
To replenish your own inner resources and develop a strong sense of personal integrity, ask yourself this question—especially if your focus is on the needs of others.

In the midst of crisis, we may suddenly come upon calm waters where the harrowing experience of uncertainty morphs into the poetry of overlapping insights into how to be present when our world has been turned upside down. This is the point at which engaging change becomes a practice in and of itself.

Here we understand that the cyclical nature of The LIGHT Process is really a lifelong work of traversing the spiral of change again and again, refining our senses and developing our ability to cross the threshold into increasingly spiritual realms of consciousness. We are gaining traction in the application of process.

Part Six: Resonance - A Port in the Storm

Our desire is to ask *What do I need right now?* from a place of heightened attunement. This is the purpose of developing emotional congruence—so that we can tune the radio receiver of self to more sublime vibrations.

Now, in moments of indecision or crisis, we come into resonance with the mature needs of our better self, rather than the petty wants of a fearful, grasping ego that can never be satisfied and that can never lead us all the way home to the fresh new tomorrow we seek.

In the center of the spiral, a portal opens upon the twist of fate we experienced earlier. Here we traverse the frontier of time and enter the timeless realms of intuition, where the question *What do I need right now?* is answered moment by moment in a perpetual conversation between attunement and wise action.

Here we experience the miracle of the fluid present as a creative space where struggle and the sense of struggle drop away. We have been making our way through the darkness and suddenly the veil parts between worlds. We have reached the eye of the hurricane.

At some point we will begin to spiral back outward, carrying the wisdom we have gained in the first half of our journey. But here we rest at the center of the storm. It is no longer a whirlwind but the deep, feminine energy of co-creativity, insight, and joyful synchronicity. We know that more turbulence awaits us, but for now all is calm and brilliantly illumined.

This is the point of balance that we enter through relaxation, trust, and a willingness to resonate with the highest good of the moment. Here is the opposite of fight-or-flight. We look with soft eyes and listen with gentle ears, sensing that the guidance we wish to follow may not be detectable if we strain after it.

What do I need right now? is a game of cosmic hide-and-seek. We are seekers for the truth of the moment, yet we are not allowed to look for it. We must simply rest in the question and allow the Universe to reveal its secrets in the nanoseconds between feeling and thought.

Insight and inspiration slip sideways into our awareness and they do it on their own terms. They can wait us out—an entire lifetime, if necessary. Our job is to meet them where they are in vibration as they resonate with the Wise Inner Counselor, who encourages us to dip into the soundless sound that is "the life of things."

A Close Call

We are not surprised when the Inner Voice instructs us to either *Get moving!* or *Wait, do nothing.* Change is replete with peaks and valleys. It is vital to detect when to stand still or when to act. Our lives may depend upon it.

I am convinced that immediately obeying a strong prompting to *Leave right now!* instead of delaying a trip to town for another two hours once saved me from veering into oncoming traffic on a two-lane country road.

Part Six: Resonance - A Port in the Storm

Looking down to change the song playing on the stereo, I lost control of my car, drove into a ditch going fast, and hit an embankment that launched my vehicle over sixty feet into an empty field where it landed hard, but flat. I was injured, but I wasn't killed—which could easily have happened if the accident had occurred at any other than the precise time and place that it did.[17]

Samantha's Story

Folded into our embrace of engaging-change-as-practice is the need to ask for help—from both seen and unseen forces. This can mean physically stopping and asking for directions. It can also mean praying for spiritual assistance when we sense that something is not right.

On a crisp, clear Friday evening in winter, Samantha (Sam to those who know her well) was driving to pick up a friend from the airport. A full moon was rising as she drove east on a busy highway, and she found herself quite concerned about the agitation she was sensing from other motorists on the road.

She could not discern if they were distracted by the spectacular sight of the enormous golden moon directly ahead, or if they were merely exhibiting the aggressive behavior that makes this road notorious for multi-car accidents.

Whatever the reason, Sam was feeling very unsettled in her body. She had long ago learned to pay attention to a sense of impending danger that registered in her gut. So she decided to pray for physical protection as she drove.

She proceeded to the airport without incident, and her friend was waiting when she pulled into the passenger pick-up area. Sam immediately turned the car around and they drove toward her friend's house, back along the same highway. Not five miles west of the airport, they noticed the eastbound traffic at a standstill behind what appeared to be a serious accident involving multiple vehicles.

Did Sam's prayers save her from that accident? These are things we will never know for sure, but Sam certainly thought they did.

The point is that the Middle of Nowhere takes on greater luminescence at its center. The path before us becomes clearer. And to expand that clarity, our need for attunement with the felt sense of circumstances as well as with the voice of the Wise Inner Counselor becomes increasingly important. The grace is that we are growing in our ability to resonate with both.

Expanding the Question

Sadly, the question *What do I need right now?* is quite easily misunderstood. Too often, need is confused with want.

Want can be an ego word—a childish demand for handouts, cushions against life's hardships, or alleviation of the responsibilities that change most certainly thrusts upon us.

Part Six: Resonance - A Port in the Storm

Need carries an entirely different connotation. It may indicate the importance of self-care—especially if others rely on our strength and clarity. When this is the case, then the question *What do I need right now?* may be considered as *What is needed of me on behalf of others?*

Throughout our lives, The LIGHT Process invites us to see ourselves as both student and teacher, especially in the midst of dramatic change. There are lessons to be learned at every turn in the road—including invitations to provide guidance to those who may be struggling with a challenge we have recently overcome.

We are presented with multiple opportunities to serve one another with compassion and loving kindness rather than acquiescing to human sympathy or the ego's whine for attention. Instead, we listen for inner guidance so that our actions are mutually enhancing to everyone involved.

From my perspective, the most important aspect of compassion as practiced by the Wise Inner Counselor is that it is always appropriate. Because the True Self has access to the All-in-all, it knows what part of universal wholeness to apply to any given situation.

The process is a bit like being a nomad whose survival depends on attunement with the shifting desert sands. Yes, there are wintering and summering areas that have consistently provided shelter and nourishment for people and animals. But a severe change in the weather can dangerously alter the landscape. Safe travel between food and water sources depends on precise reading of the signs of earth and sky. Continual adjustments and precisely timed recalculations are necessary.

This is the resonance with circumstance that the Wise Inner Counselor fosters in us on behalf of our own safe passage through life and that of those we love and support. As we learn to pay closer attention to the True Self than to the false self, we are more able to answer the call of service to others.

Gretchen's Story

Gretchen was nearly fifty years old when her desire for a better life that would also help others appeared literally out of thin air.

The divorced mother of three older teenagers, she had been working hard to support the family. Life was tough and she felt stymied in the low-paying jobs that had become her only viable source of income.

Gretchen longed for a career of more consequence for herself, her family, and the people whose lives she felt called to touch. She had been searching for new direction. But with absolutely no concept of how to go about making a change, she put the idea aside, hoping that the Universe would eventually answer her plea.

Gretchen and her son, who was twenty years old at the time, had scraped together the money to fulfill a dream

Part Six: Resonance - A Port in the Storm

they shared—to visit Nepal and experience the rarefied atmosphere of the Himalayas. She later recognized that journey as the cosmic pivot point of her life. Here's how she tells the story of the day that changed her life forever.

"It was near the end of our trip, which had been rigorous but definitely worth the effort. My son and I were on an all-day hike, high up on a spectacularly steep and rocky mountainside. Earlier in the day, we had climbed through clouds that were now hanging in a valley far below. The sky was blue above us and the thin air felt charged with energy. It was exhilarating.

"My son climbed a lookout tower about fifty feet above ground while I stayed below to meditate. Off in the distance was Mt. Everest, which we saw only briefly as the clouds parted.

"As I sat there in awe of the rugged splendor that unfolded for miles all around me, I heard an inner voice—soft at first, and then it kept 'pricking' at me. With an even, yet commandingly certain tone, it said simply, 'Go to law school.'

"I shook my head in disbelief, thinking, *Wow, the lack of oxygen must be getting to my brain.* And then I heard it again, now reverberating through my entire body: 'Go to law school.'

"This time I knew I wasn't dreaming; I was astonished! This was not how I had expected the Universe to answer my request. Both my father and brother were attorneys, but they didn't approve of women attending law school. And while my children were still living at home, I had never considered such a profession for myself.

"Besides, there were many hard-driven attorneys that I simply didn't like. To me they seemed lacking in compassion, and I didn't want to end up like that.

"As my son rejoined me, I said nothing to him. What was I going to say? My mind reeled with questions all the way down the mountain and for hours that night as I lay awake thinking, *How will my family react when I tell them? Can I even pass the entry exams?*

"Obstacles to my attending law school seemed as daunting as the Himalayan peaks. And honestly, I recoiled at the idea. *How can I possibly go to law school? I don't have enough money and besides, in terms of my being a student, I'm just too old. I've been out of school for twenty-five years.*

"Finally, just to make peace with myself and with the relentless voice in my head, I agreed to go home and take the LSAT entrance exam. At this point I wasn't willing to go to law school—only to try the exam, which I did not expect to pass.

"However, once I commit to something, I do follow through with an honest effort. After studying for several weeks, I took the LSAT and passed on the first try, at least getting a score that would qualify me for entrance. It was nothing to write home about, so I didn't tell anyone, not even my family, for fear they wouldn't be supportive.

Part Six: Resonance - A Port in the Storm

"Initially I was wait-listed by the university, which at that time meant I would be automatically admitted the following year. I applied for a scholarship and that also came through.

"While all of this was going on, I was working as a paralegal, but I was afraid of being ridiculed if I asked the attorneys in my firm to write me the required letters of recommendation. Fortunately, friends and other colleagues made sure I got the letters.

"Despite my doubts and initial resistance to the whole idea, I was going to law school!

"By now I was excited, though extremely nervous about getting started. However, once in class, I discovered that I have a talent for analysis. With plenty of study and single-minded devotion to the task at hand, understanding the law came fairly easily to me.

"I enjoyed stretching my mind. And I finally had time to do so; by now, my kids were either on their own or in college. So despite the many challenges of being an older student, I thrived at school. I met amazing instructors and fellow students who encouraged me, including a woman who has remained a dear friend and colleague.

"For about a year after graduation, I worked for several law firms. However, the jobs were not particularly enjoyable and the pay was not good. Plus, they were not really allowing me to help people other than my bosses. So I decided to open a private family law practice and manage my own schedule and client list. I was quite successful and ran that practice for nearly fifteen years.

"I'm retired now—and glad to be free of all the pressures and responsibilities. But I have to say that the work was really satisfying. It gave me a sense of purpose outside of my role as a mother. I had been very naïve when I started law school. Becoming a lawyer gave me a much stronger sense of self-worth and taught me a lot about how the world works.

"I can also see that my background as a divorced single parent gave me compassion for the struggles that couples and families face in and out of court. My knowledge and experience made a big difference for people who might otherwise have been lost in a legal system that can be terribly confusing and, at times, unkind.

"It was a long way around to be of service to others, but I don't regret the challenges I had to meet along the way. Answering that call to go to law school was one of the best decisions I ever made—for myself and for a lot of other people. It certainly wasn't the answer I expected, but I'm glad I followed the prompting.

"It's been several years since I retired, but I still get quite a few phone calls every year from former clients. They're mostly interested to learn if I'm still in practice. And they also thank me for understanding their problems and helping them get the resolution they needed."

Part Six: Resonance - A Port in the Storm

As we discover how the question *What do I need right now?* functions in our daily life, the Wise Inner Counselor is especially keen on how we work to stay grounded in the present moment.

> *The fluid present has access to all of your senses, and it plays them as if they were musical instruments.*
>
> *Your task in The LIGHT Process is to allow this music of what's happening to resonate in your body, mind, and soul so you may take the wise action that these sensations are prompting.*
>
> *The more skilled you become at noticing subtle resonance, the more smoothly will you find your way through life's changes and into your own heart. I will meet you there.*

We have reached a new phase of our experience with The LIGHT Process where a significant shift is about to take place. The level of our attunement with the Wise Inner Counselor and the degree to which we are open to the flow of events will greatly influence our ability to reconcile past and present with the future that is beginning to shine more brightly on the horizon. A new life is dawning.

Affirmation 3
Grounded in my body, I know what I need right now and what is asked of me on behalf of others.

Spiral Dancing

How do you move
    through your world?

What is the rhythm
    of your step
    or the form
    of the ripples
    you cause
    on water
    when you pass?

Spiral dancing
    flows two ways—

Into the point
    where all was dark
    and now is light
    if you will notice

Then out again,
    carrying wise words
    and Phoenix fire
    to heal
    the broken circle
    of your dreams.

If you would dance—

Learn to cultivate longing
    for the edge
    where light meets dark,
    where known meets Unknown,
    where creativity flourishes
    and the heart comes alive
    with possibility.

PART SEVEN
RECONCILIATION
Holding On and Letting Go

*Things falling apart is a kind of testing
and also a kind of healing.*

*They come together and they fall apart.
They come together again
and fall apart again.
It's just like that.*

*The healing comes
from letting there be room
for all of this to happen.*

PEMA CHÖDRON

Silent Song

Can I simply walk as a
        presence on the land?
As a soul, in fact,
        cleansed of doubt or regret

One with the rocks and grasses,
        scrubs and mossy lichens
        that do not strain against
        their lives.

They reach for the sun—
Or do they?

Perhaps they merely open
        to the sun that calls them
        to itself

Each loving each
        in mutual embrace
        and the joy of simply
        sharing a day of life
        on Planet Earth.

Is it possible to be so open
        as to hear the silent song of Presence
        caroling through the pure air,
        loving the world into being
        again and again and again?

CHAPTER 18

Finding Consolation in Our Memories

As we spiral out from the hurricane's eye, we notice that each question begins to interact more freely with the others. It becomes increasingly difficult to differentiate the tasks of one query from those of another.

Naturally, then, some aspects of *What do I need right now?* may be answered with the need for letting go or its sister undertaking of reconciliation.

Some people say they want closure after change involving loss. To me, that indicates a desire to simply make the pain go away. In reality, if a person, place, or thing has been dear to us, why would we want to be rid of the memory, even if it makes us sad? As long as that essence is alive in our hearts, it is never really lost to us.

At the end of the delightful Broadway musical *Peter and the Starcatcher* (a prequel to the story of Peter Pan), Wendy must return home to England while Peter must remain behind in Neverland with the other Lost Boys.

Finding Consolation in Our Memories

He is crying, "It hurts so bad." Wendy, who is a wise little girl, replies, "It's supposed to hurt. That's how you know it was important."

So rather than pushing away the hurt, I think what we are seeking is resolution of negative feelings and the eventual easing of sorrow through the integration of our memories. Unless we can identify and learn from the stressful meanings as well as the nurturing ones we have attached to a memory, we may lose the blessing that even a challenging recollection can offer.[18]

Chuck's Story

"I am convinced that parents and kids are destined to break each other's hearts," declared my good friend and colleague Chuck one afternoon over coffee.

Like me, Chuck is a trainer, writer, and sometime life coach. We were discussing how challenging it can be to achieve resolution with persons who are also family members. The subject clearly touched him deeply.

"My aunt has really been pushing my buttons lately," he explained, "but I think I've found some peace in the last few days,"

I knew that his aunt had raised him after his parents died when he was very young. I was also aware that their relationship was sometimes a bit fractious.

"I know she has always loved me, and I've always loved her. But she seems addicted to complaining—

Part Seven: Reconciliation - Holding On and Letting Go

especially when it comes to me," he said, as the color began to rise slightly in his cheeks.

"I know I've been a big disappointment to her for not following the traditional career path she wanted me to. And now that she's nearing the end of her life, she expects me to see her every day. Even if I wanted to, that would be unrealistic, which also disappoints her.

"I've never doubted her love for me, but the fact that she's never accepted me for who I am has made me really angry. This isn't how I want to feel about her now that she's ill, and I certainly don't want to remember her this way after she's gone."

Over the years, I have heard several friends and clients express a similar conundrum. It has been important for them to acknowledge their own disappointments, but they don't want to get stuck in that emotion—especially when it comes to people they really do love.

Since Chuck appeared to have found genuine resolution with this situation, I asked him what he did to arrive at such emotional clarity and apparent forgiveness.

He explained: "You know how we're always talking about getting our clients to tell their stories as a way of finding insight? Well, I decided to try it on myself.

"One morning I wrote down the whole story of my life with my aunt as if I were telling it in the third person.

Finding Consolation in Our Memories

This gave me some emotional distance from my interpretation, which I freely admit might not be all that accurate.

"Then, I added as many details as I could remember from events my aunt has described from her early life until I felt that somebody reading the story would get a fairly clear picture of her.

"It's funny, really. I've been telling the tale of our life together for years, but I'd never written it down. There was something about putting it on paper and then reading it as if it belonged to somebody else that showed me how her personality and behaviors made perfect sense.

"I may not have appreciated her opinion of what I should do with my life, but within the context of her upbringing and the historical events she lived through, she did her best. And under the circumstances, her best was really pretty good."

Chuck knows how much I like asking questions to process personal issues, so I smiled when he admitted (with a twinkle in his eye) that inquiry has become his new favorite process of self-reflection.

He continued: "With this feeling of acceptance in mind, I was then able to ask myself some tough questions about my own thoughts and feelings toward my aunt.

- What have I learned from her?
- What has our relationship meant to me?
- How I am allowing that memory to sit in me?
- Is it moving me forward or holding me back?

Part Seven: Reconciliation ~ Holding On and Letting Go

- What part did I play in creating the difficulties between us?
- Can I forgive her for being human?
- And can I forgive myself for my own failings, vulnerabilities, and lack of kindness?

"As I considered our years together, especially the personal sacrifice she made to take me in after my parents died, I felt real gratitude for her—and something in me relaxed. Regardless of whether or not we could accept one another's reasons, I had to admit that we each did the best we could at the time.

"Accepting responsibility for my own actions and refusing to feel guilt or regret made it much easier for me to open my heart. In fact, I began to experience a sort of exhilaration as more questions popped into my head.

- Can I move on from here?
- Can I replace troubling emotions with gratitude for the lessons I most likely would not have learned any other way?
- Are there any memories that I still cherish because they are happy and/or the source of enormous insight into my own life?

"This is really hard to admit, but I used to think that my aunt had to pass away for me to feel that I was free of her disappointment along with my own guilt that I couldn't be the person I have to be for myself as well as

Finding Consolation in Our Memories

the one she wanted me to be for her. That's not true anymore. After asking myself all these questions, I really have forgiven both of us. It's as if a huge weight is just gone."

My eyes filled with tears as Chuck declared the honest joy that accepting himself and his aunt had brought him. As I reflected on my own relationships, it occurred to me that our memories are highly interdependent.

We know that others teach us—and we them. I proposed to Chuck that we also teach ourselves.

"I agree," he said with a nod. "In fact, this is an exercise I'm going to use with my clients. I keep coming up with more questions, and I'd like to see how other people answer them.

- What am I teaching myself through my memories?
- Are they lessons of growth or limitation, love or fear?
- How might I reframe them into useful lessons?
- How might I move forward if memories that used to be challenging were now free of their negative emotional charge?"

As Chuck left the coffee shop to attend another meeting, I sat a while longer, absorbing the implications of the deep emotional work he had shared with me.

I think his final question is the real key to knowing when we have achieved resolution with a memory that

Part Seven: Reconciliation - Holding On and Letting Go

may lead to reconciliation with another person—and with our own self-image.

When I asked what real forgiveness feels like, here is the explanation my Wise Inner Counselor offered:

> *Forgiveness feels like something that was never there. The act of forgiving withdraws the negative emotional energy from a recollection so that it can no longer move you.*

I guess it's like my mother saying to my father as he was dying, "We'll just remember the good things, not the things that went wrong." And he said to her, "Did anything go wrong?"

Fire Ceremony

Meet me on the Other Side, he said,
    and I will show you
    what it's like
    to rest in Light

There's something
    that you need to know
    about the past that blocks—

An ancient fear of dreams
    you've spent your
    whole life running from

Sit still, my love, by water's edge,
    and do not resist the deep
    that calls you forth

You have the power
    at your fingertips,
    the wisdom
    in your garments

The underground seed
    is nearly set to bloom,
    but the old ways must go

You are so much more
> than anyone's opinion

Die the good death
> to all that is false,
>> and be transition's offspring

A fire is coming
> and it will shake you
> to your core

The Phoenix bird is rising.

CHAPTER 19

Releasing the Albatross

By the time we have become grounded in our bodies and attuned to what is most appropriate and necessary for us in the present moment, we begin to notice that certain outworn patterns of thinking, feeling, and behaving start falling away. Rather than asking *What do I need to let go of?* the question has flipped into *What is letting go of me?*

The keenest entrepreneurs among us are masters of knowing when to let go. These folks seem to carry in their genes a unique, inborn sense of non-attachment that informs everything they do.

Taylor is the perfect example of such a person. In reality, he is a composite, not a real person. But his story is absolutely true because he represents an entire tribe of transition leaders.

These are the idea people—the early adopters—inventors, artists, parents, lawyers, business owners, and others who are always on the lookout for what's

Part Seven: Reconciliation ~ Holding On and Letting Go

next. In many cases, they are the ones who create the next big thing. These innovators from every walk of life see tomorrow as if it were today and then go about inventing that future for the rest of us.

Some of them are my best friends. Others have been the most challenging bosses I ever worked for. Still others are thought leaders I greatly admire. On my best days, I count myself among them.

The point is that these innovation enthusiasts are always nudging the status quo to either get moving or move over. They are compelled to continue in their life's work as co-creators with the universal force whose first principle is to lovingly extend itself outward in new growth.

For the purposes of this story, Taylor is a man. He could just as easily be cast as a woman, as are many of the entrepreneurs I have known. In either case, what is particularly notable about the core virtue of these individuals is their dynamic balance of masculine and feminine energy that combines the ability to see things as they are with imagining what they could be.

These are the natural change agents who sometimes alchemize a situation merely by entering a room. Like walking paradoxes, they are wise and childlike, reserved and boldly assertive.

And they understand in their bones what tribe member Pablo Picasso meant when he reportedly said, "Each act of creation is first of all an act of destruction."

Taylor's Story

Taylor is an innovator and a business entrepreneur. A quintessential idea person, he works a lot like Thomas Edison, who imagined his inventions from every possible angle, including from the inside out.

Once Taylor has gathered every available fact about the new project he is working on, he spends days, weeks, or sometimes months twisting, turning, supposing, and imagining how his idea might work.

At a certain point, he takes a break from all of this vigorous brainstorming. Often a nap is enough[19] or a good night's sleep. At other times Taylor takes an entire weekend off. The duration is not particularly important. What's key is the complete exhaustion to which he has subjected his brain in what can appear to others as mindless play.

During this interval, Taylor purposefully does no ruminating until the *aha!* moment when a golden idea appears, often with a felt sense that he can hear as well as feel. Sometimes an idea will be so vivid that all of Taylor's senses are triggered.

Once inspiration has struck, it is a relatively simple task to unpack the details of the idea and put them into action—of course with the caveat that simple does not equal easy. Developing a new project can involve many cycles of trial and error, which Taylor also enjoys.

Without fail, soon after all systems are running smoothly, Taylor will suddenly announce, "I'm done!"

Part Seven: Reconciliation - Holding On and Letting Go

This is his sign to let somebody else take the reins of daily operations so he can get back to his job of innovation. In fact, he is famous with his friends for declaring, "I don't do maintenance."

A few years ago, Taylor had an epiphany. The company he and a partner had started was wildly successful. They were making more money than they ever dreamed possible and their product was helping hundreds of professionals to be more effective.

For the first time in his life, Taylor was considering holding on to a company instead of selling it and moving ahead with the next project. This was highly unusual because, like most entrepreneurs, he relished developing a project more than the project itself.

On the day of Taylor's epiphany, he was driving to his office along the road he had traveled almost daily for the past year. It was a familiar route that required only partial attention to navigate—or so he thought.

Suddenly, an enormous dog ran out in front of him. Slamming on the breaks and swerving to avoid hitting it, he lost control of the car, spun around, and came to rest at a ninety-degree angle from where he had been headed.

I guess it's time to change direction, thought Taylor as he gratefully realized that neither he nor his car had sustained damage from this encounter with destiny. Once he arrived at work later that morning he took immediate steps to divest himself of managerial responsibilities and sell his share of the company.

This accident was one of many signs from the Unseen that Taylor had followed throughout his career. What was special about this rather dramatic warning was the insight it provided into a level of resistance that he had not previously acknowledged.

"It was as if selling this company meant giving up one of my kids," Taylor mused after the accident. "When you give birth to a new project, nurturing it from fledgling to full flight, it's hard not to become emotionally attached. I fall in love with my innovations like a parent does with his or her children.

"What was remarkable about the jolt I got from this accident was that I saw how I also fall in love with the person I am when I'm creating. And because every innovation is unique, so is that manifestation of myself.

"So every time I sell one of my companies, I lose both the metaphorical child and its parent—the particular Taylor who will never again show up in quite the same way. I suppose I've always known this, but I had resisted facing the sense of loss until now.

"When I was younger, I just zipped from one creative project to the next. Now that I'm further along in my career, I guess I count the cost of change more realistically. In fact, I never understood there was a cost. Now I do.

Part Seven: Reconciliation - Holding On and Letting Go

"When I sold this last company, I did something I have never done before: I acknowledged that I have some grief over moving forward. Even though I'm excited about the new ideas I'm working on, I have allowed myself to experience that bit of sadness that was always there.

"And you know what? Giving myself permission to grieve has freed up my creative juices for the next really cool invention.

"It's almost as if I had been carrying around bits of unresolved sorrow for all of the companies I had created and then sold over the years. That blocked energy was becoming an albatross around my neck. I couldn't see it, but it was beginning to affect my creativity.

"Now that I've released it, I've got ideas popping so fast I can hardly keep up with them. I never would have realized any of this except for that crazy dog that sent me spinning in a new direction."

So for the many Taylors out there and for the bit of Taylor's spirit that resides in each of us, I believe we need to embrace the idea of impermanence. We do not own our creations any more than parents own their children. At some point, we must release them into the world. And if we are to discover our own way forward in life, doing so will be one of the best decisions we will ever make.

CHAPTER 20

Viewing Impermanence as Natural

Question 4: What do I need to let go of?
Even positive change can be accompanied by elements of loss and grief. Ask this question to help yourself open to the possibility of releasing what is naturally falling away.

A powerful myth about change is that it will eventually lead to stability. That we'll return to some type of familiar normalcy or perhaps discover a new one. That we will catch a break, maybe even a little beach time, before life's next surprise. In my experience, that is mostly not true.

In fact, it seems that the more facile one becomes with surfing the waves of transition, the harder and faster they come. People of all ages agree: we are living in an age of unprecendented acceleration.

The LIGHT Process invites us to accept ambiguity as the true norm. Despite our reliance on familiar patterns and habits as buttresses against the ebb and flow of the natural world, life is a perpetual conversation between conflicting experiences: ruts and realizations, obstacles and opportunities.

Our job is to flow with this paradox in profound understanding that balance does not mean stasis. Standing upright on one foot requires many micro-adjustments all the way up one's leg. Likewise, change is the multi-layered rule of life—not the exception.

Life as a Sand Painting

I was never drawn to acting in film or on television. Instead, I loved the excitement of performing for a live audience. Part of the thrill was the challenge of making a production new every night, even after dozens of repetitions.

The experience was poignant because, after every performance, the show disappeared. We began in a dark theater and ended in one. In between was pure magic and, eight times a week, each event was a little different.

We expect this kind of impermanence from a live show, but for some reason we don't expect it from life. We grieve when things change.

Like exquisite sand paintings that are painstakingly produced and then purposefully destroyed by shamans and monks from many spiritual traditions,[20] the more elaborately we create our human constructs, the greater is the potential for events that change them to seem cruelly destructive. If we try to codify or artificially preserve

Viewing Impermanence as Natural

these beautiful structures, we are even more vulnerable to suffering when they pass away.

We in the West are highly susceptible to this agony because we view change as loss. Eastern and tribal traditions are more likely to view transition as opportunity for openness. And therein lies the secret of knowing when to hold on and when to let go.

The other day I came upon an apt phrase in a book on Native American spirituality. The author talks about releasing anything that "no longer grows corn for you."[21]

My Wise Inner Counselor immediately joined the discussion:

> *This is an important key. If a person, place, or thing is still alive in your life in a way that adds to your joyful engagement and progress, then it is good to hold it close.*
>
> *But if its presence has become an empty husk that is no longer capable of growth, let it naturally fall away. And as it slips into dust, open your heart to the new shoots poking their heads up to take its place.*
>
> *This is the way of Nature. It is the way of change.*

A Gift of Many Blessings

In her exquisite book *Broken Open: How Difficult Times Help Us Grow*, Elizabeth Lesser says it this way: "The promise of being broken and the possibility of being opened are written into the contract of human life."[22]

As I apply Lesser's assertion in my own life, I sense

Part Seven: Reconciliation - Holding On and Letting Go

that transition's wounds are what have made me open, emotionally available, and more compassionate toward others and myself. As long as I can allow each subsequent "old self" to be burned up in the alchemical fires of change, there is always hope for my truer, more authentic, more resilient Self to emerge from the ashes of experience.

These realizations do not come easily. As anyone who is familiar with my work on grief will attest, losing my beloved husband was the worst thing that ever happened to me. It is also the most important because of who I have become and what I have learned in the process of profound mourning and my even deeper determination to rebuild a life that I had to learn to want.

Gratitude for being stripped of people and things that I have loved has been hard won—and it is genuine. Not because I loved so little, but because I loved so much.

The experience of loss has opened my heart to the concept of impermanence. I have come to realize that what change snatched away from me has mysteriously become part of who and what I am. I have internalized the lover I lost, the parent I always wanted, the actualized Self I used to admire in others.

This integration of what is truly important in my life has allowed me to metaphorically die to those issues that no longer grow corn for me. With gratitude for the lessons I have learned while in relationship to various beloveds, I am now able to acknowledge and then transcend my past rather than negating or clinging to it.

Meditation and a lifelong practice of listening for inner guidance have taught me to raise areas of internal incompleteness up to the light rather than pushing them into psychic shadows. I have learned that allowing them to rattle around in my subconscious, agitating for attention, makes resolving them much more difficult to accomplish the next time they surface.

So while an issue is still current or when an old one is up, I deal with it. And when I have needed the assistance of professional counseling, I have pursued it.

Powerful change has a way of bringing long-forgotten memories to the surface, where they can be dealt with by the conscious mind. But after the sublime discovery of partnership with the Divine, it can be shocking to find ourselves once again in the dark of emotions we would prefer not to deal with.

This is not necessarily cause for alarm. Issues of the past do surface and resurface as a natural activity of The LIGHT Process. We can even interpret this arising as progress. Often these deep memories are not released until we have learned to function from the strength of our core virtue, with the added support of centering practice and the loving presence of the Wise Inner Counselor.

However, I have found that a qualified therapist who

Part Seven: Reconciliation - Holding On and Letting Go

understands how to work with disturbing emotions can offer a stabilizing perspective. Personally, I have found that these bedrock issues are best not tackled alone.

At times I have been shocked at the smallness of my human consciousness that reveals itself. Fortunately, with experience and the occasional skillful counseling session, I have trained myself to embrace deep issues when they come to light.

I now know to integrate the lessons these shadowy elements carry in their deep recesses of illusion. And I lovingly accept these formerly rejected aspects of being—now freed of guilt or blame or fear—back into the fold of my conscious awareness.[23]

Thanks to having been broken open by change, when I now find myself sinking below the waves of attachment, I can take a deep breath and ask, *What am I afraid of?*—which is often code for *What am I afraid of losing?*

When I follow that fear to its source, I often discover that what I am really afraid of is not what I originally thought. In fact, a surface fear sometimes obscures hidden treasure. Being open to that possibility has proved to be a gift that offers many blessings.

I believe that as we reach the end of this phase of The LIGHT Process we are no longer trying to resolve our problems at the level at which they occurred. We have gone far beyond them. And in the process, we have increased what I call our *refract-ability*. We have become more refined crystals of being, containing myriad facets with which to catch and emit the light of our True Self.

That is what being open demonstrates as it carries us to a new tomorrow that we never could have imagined when change first interrupted us on our way to wherever it was we thought we were going.

Affirmation 4
Healing happens when I open up, and I am finding a way to be grateful for the experiences that caused the opening.

Buena Vista

Driving across
      a great expanse of valley
The soul's eye reaches out
      to touch the landscape
And the heart declares,
      "I am ready."

PART EIGHT
RESILIENCE
Bending in the Wind

*The green reed that bends in the wind
is stronger than the mighty oak
that breaks in a storm.*

CONFUCIUS

What to Expect from Life

Expect the unexpected
>but do not watch for it.

It's shy
>and does not wish to be seen
>until you have forgotten to look.

Transformation will come
>when you give up trying.

Power may be given,
>but only from the inside out.

Meaning shifts and shapes
>around your changes,
>and peace tiptoes in
>by hindsight.

Life is a disappearing act
>practiced by travelers
>fond of losing their way.

CHAPTER 21

Following the Omens

Years ago, my book group read Paulo Coelho's classic tale *The Alchemist*. Early in the story, a mysterious old man advises the protagonist that in order to find the treasure he seeks, he must "follow the omens."

The old man explains that there is a benign universal force that wants each of us to achieve our personal destiny. There is a path to that outcome, and it is laced with cosmic signposts that can only be seen by those whose hearts are open to partnership with Nature and the Divine.

This admonition became a guiding principle for me and two other readers in that book group. Although we read *The Alchemist* years ago, we still marvel at the miracles of synchronicity that have occurred in our lives since we decided to pay attention to the signs and way-showers that are often right in front of us.

In many cases, those external guides have merely confirmed the intuitive direction we had already received.

Sometimes flashes of inspiration are so subtle that we can miss them. But when they are reinforced by the sudden appearance of an outer sign that we have learned to take as a message, then we know to either act immediately or stay put until circumstances have evolved.

Sometimes the direction is to remain silent; at other times the strong prompting is to speak up—to say the thing that has just come to mind.

The Contractor's Story

"Isn't it amazing how things just work out when you're open to them?"

That's what the young contractor said to me as we were discussing the repair of a window in my house that had leaked over the winter.

"I've been wanting to get back into meditation; I can feel myself slipping. If I don't do it every day, pretty soon I'm all wrapped up in my head, trying to control my life. And then things just stop working the way they should. But if I pay attention to the little promptings, everything seems to fall into place.

"A buddy of mine says it's not the big problems that get you, it's the mosquito bites. You know, the little irritations, the missed connections, the small stumbles.

"What's incredible is that just the other day I was really frustrated, so I asked the Universe to get me back on track. And now we're having this conversation.

Part Eight: Resilience - Bending in the Wind

"It's amazing—except that it isn't, really. This is how things work if I let them."

As often happens, our connection had begun quite simply. The contractor was trying to figure out when to have a drywall specialist come over to fix my windowsill.

I explained that he could come over any time because I work from home as a writer. The contractor wanted to know what I write and then told me about a friend of his who is in transition and wants to devote full time to writing.

I told him the story of my late husband, whose path of self-realization was centered in deep meditation. And off we went into one of those magical dialogs that feel like cosmic set-ups.

I gave him a copy of my first book.[24] I knew without a doubt that the story of another man's journey through life was exactly the inspiration this bright young fellow needed. In the space of ten minutes, our two lives had been enriched for many days to come—all because I followed through when my intuition told me to explain that I am a writer who works from home.

This is how I have learned to bend in the winds of change. Nowadays I follow the omens even when they are nothing more than a ripple on the surface of awareness. I have learned not to be bashful about mentioning some aspect of my work to people who serendipitously enter my life. Time after time—on airplanes, in grocery stores, at the bank, signing up for car insurance, or meeting with a financial planner—my experience has been exactly what they needed to hear.

More often than not, these connections occur at the exact moment when they were searching for an answer or point of inspiration that would move them onward in their journey of self-discovery.

And the other lovely thing is that when I need to be inspired, somebody or something invariably shows up in my life to provide the exact impetus necessary to boost me forward on my own path.

So I have learned not to be silent. It is part of the contract of mutual trust I have with the Universe. When I pay attention and speak up, miracles of connection take place. In fact, I still have a vision board that contains the directive "Speak up! The world is listening." I do my best to take that admonition to heart every day.

CHAPTER 22

Creating a Better Tomorrow

We are a hopeful species. We expect that tomorrow will be better than today. We have a sense of living in an abundant, ever-expanding, inexhaustibly creative universe. So we instinctively anticipate improvement.

Nature is likewise optimistic. It is the very essence of persistently positive intention. Just consider a tree growing out of a hairline crack in a solid rock wall or a site as awe-inspiring as the Grand Canyon. Nature moves relentlessly toward a new and improved future—even if it takes millions of years to form.

We are the heirs of this positivity, and part of our inheritance is to continue its work. The foundational principle of this labor is that tomorrow will unfold according to the intentions we hold for it.

This is how we make our own good fortune—we create mental patterns called thought-forms that attract cosmic energy to fill them in.

I recall Tibetan Lama Sogyal Rinpoche saying, "If you would know your past, look to your present circumstances. If you would know your future, look to your present thoughts."[25]

If this is true, then tomorrow becomes a self-fulfilling prophecy that is based on what we envision today. It is the stuff of Story Three, the new story that we considered early in The LIGHT Process. Now we go about consciously writing that narrative from the place of mental, emotional, and spiritual clarity that we experienced while in the eye of transition's whirling storm.

By now, we have come to realize that the essence of living on the razor's edge of change is not so much what we do at any point in time, but rather how we show up for what is happening in that moment.

Where we once tried to bend circumstances to our will, now we see that true power is not force. We are reminded of great T'ai Chi or Aikido masters who can fell an opponent with the flick of a finger, and we determine to be likewise centered and energetically economical.

Although forceful external events may have precipitated the upheavals we have experienced, the internal transformation we seek is effected through a gentle overcoming of fear, even a playful spirit that flows from compassion for others and patience with self—and above all, from acknowledging that each of us matters because we are here.[26]

Part Eight: Resilience - Bending in the Wind

We live in a power-mad world, but Nature's message is that change cannot be forcibly grasped. Our task in this life is to continually find creative ways in which to reflect and internalize its movement.

When we truly see into the life of things, we notice that Nature is forever synthesizing what came before into a new manifestation that matches the ongoing need for adaptive growth. This is progress, and we are called to emulate it.

Each cycle includes and transcends the one that preceded it, always adding its own creative spin that makes it unique from every other spiral that has gone before. A fresh rose unfolds in the same spiraling pattern as does every previous rose, and yet no two are alike.

This natural action is the spirit of resilient novelty. And we are just loaded with it. Opening our hearts to a creative future is one of the most important outcomes of The LIGHT Process, for here we find a fountain of individual and collective freedom that, once unleashed, cannot be denied. The challenge is to release it with positive intentions and good will toward all.

Dennis's Story

My father, Dennis, came from a long line of pioneers. His Irish ancestors, the Laffertys, were a particularly restless bunch with a love of the frontier in their blood. Always inspired by the vision of a better tomorrow, they kept heading west—emigrating from Ireland to William Penn's American colony in the late 1700s, with branches of the family eventually ending up in Colorado and California in the 1940s.

Although he never attended college, Dennis was also a pioneer in his career as an electrical engineer. While in high school in the late 1930s, he became fascinated by crystal radio technology and apprenticed himself to a man who owned the latest equipment.

After the attack on Pearl Harbor when the United States entered World War II, Dennis was able to apply his knowledge of crystal radios and qualify for training with the U. S. Army Signal Corps.[27] This technical services arm of the U. S. Army Air Corps was turning out radio engineers as fast as it could to meet wartime demand. So immediately upon graduation, Dennis got a job that lasted through 1945.

For several years after the war, he taught electronics to airmen returning from active duty and then ran a radio repair business with a buddy. Always eager to try out the latest electronics, Dennis bought one of the first black-and-white consumer television sets available in the early 1950s. When the opportunity presented itself, he jumped at the chance to become a TV repairman.

In the early 1960s the Martin Marietta Company brought the space program to Denver, and Dennis was one of their first new hires. As a technical training instructor, he wrote and taught courses on logistics for the Titan

Part Eight: Resilience - Bending in the Wind

missile program and later for the space shuttle. All of the projects he worked on were classified, so he couldn't talk about them at home. But it was clear that he loved being part of this new frontier.

Of course, a lifetime spent following technology's lead was not without its difficulties. In a dramatic event during WWII, a serious challenge arose from individuals who did not share my father's commitment to integrity, preferring instead to take shortcuts for expediency and profit.

Dennis had been assigned as an on-site Air Corps quality control specialist at the manufacturing plant of a firm that made crystals for radios in military aircraft. Unfortunately, the crystals in the planes used in the Pacific Theater of Operations were getting wet and failing, often when the pilots were flying around islands with miles of ocean in between.

The situation was dire but was being remedied by gold plating the crystals to seal out the moisture. However, Dennis quickly discovered that the company was cutting corners, diminishing the quality of the gold plating and then trying to ship defective crystals. They were putting hundreds of pilots in jeopardy. As the only safeguard between the company and the airmen, Dennis knew what he had to do.

For me and others who are familiar with his strong sense of integrity, it is not hard to picture him informing

Creating a Better Tomorrow

the company supervisors that he would not approve their product until significant changes were made. But, at the time, I'm sure the heavyweights with money on the line were completely flummoxed by the determination of this soft-spoken young man who stood barely five and a half feet tall and never weighed more than one hundred thirty pounds.

They threatened to have him fired or replaced, but he stood his ground and told them to call his boss at the Air Corps. Confident of their position, they did so. Fortunately for all concerned, the military brass agreed with my father, and the gold plating was brought up to the proper safety standard.

Apparently quality was never again an issue at that company, and Dennis went on to serve in a similar capacity at various installations around the country. The Air Corps knew they could depend on him to hold the line, even under extreme pressure not to.

This is how my mother told the story. My father was a deeply spiritual man who rarely talked about himself. He has been deceased for many years, so I can't ask him for more details about this experience.

Still, I wonder if he ever thought about how very differently the future would have unfolded if he had not held true to his integrity and dedication to creating the best possible tomorrow for himself and for all those who depended on him.

Part Eight: Resilience - Bending in the Wind

The Wise Inner Counselor comments:

To achieve the tomorrow you want, you must first create the image in your mind and hold it in your heart. Thoughts of inferiority create inferior forms, so focus on elevated intentions.

It is important to perfect the crystal of consciousness. The chalice must be able to hold more spiritual energy tomorrow than it does today.

Move forward into the light of your being. See it. Feel it. Accept it. Use it and it will only increase. Do not limit the potential of the Divine that lives in your heart.

Tomorrow unfolds according to your loyalty to your own True Self. If you had any idea of who and what you really are, you would not doubt. You would run to greet that Self at dawn, rejoicing in each new day of creative opportunity.

When such feelings begin at home, the entire world is blessed.

When Things Won't Change

'Tis easy to miss it—
    the little bit that happens
    when things won't change.

The imperceptible flutter
    of a butterfly's wing
    that is the bit that's moving
    when things won't change.

Life is not all dust and stasis
    even when things feel stuck.

Only love's eye
    detects a breeze
    as soft as baby's breath
    blowing you along.

Sometimes to move forward
    you have to go back
    and pick up what or whom
    you forgot to love

Or fall in love
    all over again,
    remembering
    what first drew you
    to this place or to that one.

We love for many reasons.
Finding out why again
    may be the bit that's moving
    when things don't appear
    to change.

And when you let that
    forgotten love back in,
    you may come to see
    that change has been
    there all along.

CHAPTER 23

Love, Acceptance, and Joy

We don't get through anything truly difficult except by embracing the challenge and accepting the joy that lies behind the impediment we perceive. When life backs us into a corner and refuses to budge, we must be the ones to blink—because there is a purpose here.

Of course, we can cop out in the short term, avoiding the problem, taking what we think is the safe way out, allowing fear of what is unknown and doubt in our talents to sabotage us. But the Universe sees through our shenanigans and will not allow us to move on until we have learned the lesson before us.

So unless we choose to continue running into the same brick walls—situation after situation—we will summon the courage to confront these obstacles face to face. At a certain point, we must discover the thin place that is the way through them. We will find it in love.

Part Eight: Resilience - Bending in the Wind

Ultimately, life comes down to a simple question: *How well have you loved?* When we have landed in a tight spot where circumstances are not going well—or at least not to our liking—the answer to that ultimate question may be: *Not well enough. Not humbly enough. Not with sufficient compassion. Not in a spirit of joyful acceptance.*

It is the false self that persists in demanding how, when, or where change should occur. But the ego cannot comprehend that the creative tension at the heart of metamorphosis will not release until the butterfly is fully formed in its chrysalis.

The next phase of transition will unfold as do the butterfly's wings. Bit by bit, the gorgeous creature gains strength by straining to break free of its filmy bonds. We cannot rush its liberation, for a cycle is not finished until Nature has had its due.

The natural world is patient. So is the loving Spirit that guides us humans through our own transformation. The Wise Inner Counselor is relentless in its desire to turn our attention inward to an awareness of divine intention and good will.

So when things won't change, the answer is to stop looking for external troubles to correct. Eventually, the trail of physical causes runs cold and we are left with a choice: Look within and trust that love is the source of all remedies. Or remain stuck in a rigid suffering of our own creation. The Wise Inner Counselor says:

Love, Acceptance, and Joy

> *The way to prime the pump of change is to bloom where you're planted. Put down roots as if you could live there forever, and suddenly, you may not have to. With your attention on growth, new life can emerge. All that was missing was your engagement with circumstances as they are, even when they are painfully imperfect.*

The Way of Nature

I suspect most people would say that acceptance is a result of love. Recently, however, I have come to believe that acceptance comes first. Real, unselfish love of another flows from true and abiding acceptance of that person's unique traits—not in spite of them.

All too often it seems that modern couples fall in love and then, before long, at least one of the partners embarks on a serious remodeling campaign to turn the one they had initially seen as flawless into an entirely different person.

It is one thing to enter into mutual agreement to help one another grow in wisdom and compassion. It is quite a different matter to have designs on someone that have little to do with the True Self that he or she is becoming.

During one of my many car trips between Montana and Colorado, it occurred to me that unconditional self-acceptance is the way of Nature. The mountain does not wish to be a valley. Rocks seem quite content to be rocks. Fish do not pine for wings, and birds do not yearn to gallop over the plains like wild mustangs.

Part Eight: Resilience - Bending in the Wind

At the root of such deep acceptance of the "is-ness" of things is a universal trust that all is in divine order. When we allow ourselves to look behind change, we may discover that even unwelcome circumstances can contain hidden opportunities for profound transformation.[28]

When we can accept that cycles which appear flawed may be merely incomplete, we relax. Doubt flees, and the pure, resilient joy of being alive dissolves the ego's mental and emotional wrangling after solutions that are actually still in process.

When we allow ourselves to sink into deep, grounded presence by lovingly accepting what is or is not happening, we may be surprised to find that what bubbles up around us is the perfect joy that transcends doubt and fear.

The Wise Inner Counselor comments:

> *To be truly joyful is to be free of doubt and fully engaged in each day—not as if it were your last, but as if it were your first, marvelous, astonishing moment of realization that you are alive and present—here, now, today.*
>
> *If you would be healed of the wounds that are often opened by change or the lack of change, love people and situations as they are. Unconditional acceptance that there are larger forces at work than may be immediately apparent is the key that unlocks the door to the Beautiful Middle of Now Here.*

CHAPTER 24

Fulfilling the Heart's Desires

Question 5: Where do I go from here?
As a result of your transformative experiences on the spiral of change, a world of creative potential opens up when you ask yourself this final question.

Once more we have an opportunity to reframe a question. In this case, *Where do I go from here?* flips into *What is calling me forward into a new, more resilient life?*

When we have been fully engaged in the previous four questions—allowing their sister affirmations to bloom in us—the final phase of The LIGHT Process becomes one of delicious discovery. Rather than stressing over five- or ten-year plans that we must will into manifestation, we open our hands to gifts of synchronicity that a generous Universe is all too happy to bestow upon us.

Of course, we work to be in the right place at the right time in the right state of mind. We live wisely. We

Part Eight: Resilience - Bending in the Wind

love generously and we allow ourselves to be deeply touched by the losses that inevitably visit us.

We take precautions. We do not tempt fate with foolish get-rich-quick schemes. We fulfill our obligations to family, career, and community. And we do not put our faith in outer things that can never fill the bottomless pit of the ego's belief in scarcity.

We live within our means and prioritize our actions according to how they contribute to compassion for self and others. And we pay attention to our heart's desires—allowing them to lead us on in joyful fulfillment of our reason for being.

I do believe that the heart's deepest desires are put there by the Divine. The longing for love, for meaningful work, for companionship, for oneness—even the need for comfort and play—all these are part of Spirit's longing in us. Not wants, which are based on lack, but *de-sires*, the longings that are sired by Deity.

However, just because these yearnings are lawful does not mean that the timetable of their fulfillment is up to us. On the contrary, the deeper and more meaningful the hunger, the less likely are we able to satisfy it on our own terms or expectations.

Because our heart's desires flow from the Divine, the timeline for their fulfillment is also Spirit-directed.

Eternally connected to the Divine's dream for each of us, the Wise Inner Counselor knows more about aspiration's purpose than we do. It comprehends more about our destiny than we will ever see.

It is more concerned with journey than with destination. And it is more focused on what we learn and how we love along the way than with how quickly we reach a goal—even a divinely inspired one.

In fact, just to slow us down, our Wise Inner Counselor may allow obstacles to spring up in our path. It says:

> *Stop and tend the roses. Connect with life along the way. Learn to accept yourself, so that when the object of your desire comes along, you will no longer see your goal as something external.*
>
> *It will no longer be a thing to be obtained; the essence of that which is desired will have already found its way into your being. You will attract it to yourself because you already contain it—whether it is the love of your life, the work you were born to do, or a spiritual connection that is the foundation of all other desires.*

In other words, these things that we desire will no longer be objects. They will have become energetic manifestations of love that find further expression in the fulfillment of our desired outcome.

Part Eight: Resilience - Bending in the Wind

If I have learned anything from The LIGHT Process, it is that there are no shortcuts. In fact, when I have tried to cut across the spiral, it seems to have grown wider. I know that I have actually lengthened the time necessary to attain certain goals when I have acted as if I were in charge of my life.

None of us is in charge. We do not possess our lives. We can only own our choices and their consequences. Ultimately, we are the progeny of a benign Universe that *is* in charge and yet does not force the relationship.

Opportunity is offered with the promise of a path that leads to authentic power, meaning, and peace. Our choice lies in whose direction we follow while making the journey.

Power, Meaning, and Peace

Tomorrow slips in through the cracks. We do not transform ourselves. We allow a mysterious process to work in and through us. New ideas come of their own accord, not because we force them. Even the most skilled creative thinkers know that they are powerless to do other than fashion the environment that welcomes new ideas.

Such is the true nature of power, meaning, and peace. They are gentle gifts that unfold as a reward for paying attention to life. And they emerge from paradox.

Real power arises when one does not desire it. Meaning that heals comes from allowing the question

Fulfilling the Heart's Desires

to sit in us. Lasting peace emerges when all thoughts of attack cease, when the desire for supremacy has faded into emptiness, and we are left in a calm and loving acceptance of what is.

We do not grasp after divine inspiration. We do not mount a frontal assault. We approach from the oblique. We enter willingly into the rich darkness of ambiguity with only five core questions as our guide. We work and then we rest, knowing that insight often comes when we look away.

It is possible to emerge from the turmoil of the Middle of Nowhere and forget how courageous we have been on our journey. I suppose it's a bit like childbirth. Once the pain stops and you behold the miracle that life has wrought, it is hard not to think of the process as magical.

Of course, it is not—which is one reason for taking time to reflect on how much progress we have made. A new tomorrow will unfold according to the level of our engagement in the previous phases. It is natural to the extent that we take advantage of a cosmic spin afforded by letting go of outworn patterns and opening up to new possibility.

We must be fully committed to our present life if we are to be deeply transformed in the process of transcending it. It is not possible to dissolve the human ego until you have built a solid sense of self. As psychologist Jack Engler once quipped, "You have to be somebody before you can be nobody."[29] The same is true here: We cannot transcend a life we have not cherished.

When we exercise continued courage to step out into the richness of being present in our own lives, we find that that's where the juice is. Living in this place of serendipitous connection ultimately transforms our experience with change into one of profound insight.

We feel powerful because we are no longer victims of loss. Life has meaning because it contains renewed purpose—even if that purpose is as simple as deciding to relish all of life, rough patches as well as smooth ones. And we are at peace because we know that we work in partnership with benevolent, unseen forces.

Transformation is a daily occurrence because we pay attention to our inner guidance with gratitude for the inspiration that flows to us.

Still, the Wise Inner Counselor reminds us:

> *As you anticipate a brighter tomorrow, don't be alarmed if it arrives with change in its pocket, tossing you once more into the Middle of Nowhere.*
>
> *And don't be surprised if you find the event shocking. Somehow, humans are always taken aback when things change. Yet the truth of The LIGHT Process is that life will rarely be so tidy as to let you complete one whole spiral before spinning you out into several more.*

So when your existence is once more disrupted, your plans dashed, and your hopes again delayed, ask yourself five simple questions and do the deep personal work from which the affirmations emerge.

With diligent engagement in the peaks and valleys of change, Nowhere will eventually tip into Now Here. And you will know it as the most beautiful place on earth.

Affirmation 5
*Tomorrow unfolds as naturally as I allow—
and I am allowing myself to be divinely directed.*

The Wild

I knew her once,
    The Wild.

The one who lived free
    in exuberant joy,
        in love with being here.

Fearless, sunny—
    a light that shone
    on all she met
    and welcomed
    what might come.

What must fall away
    to get her back?

Only blinders, perhaps,
    or doubt—
        more likely lack of trust
        in her reality.

She was never really far away,
    needing only
    a gentle invitation
    to reappear.

PART NINE
RENAISSANCE
The Beautiful Middle of Now Here

*Be alert for any sign of beauty or grace.
Offer up every joy.
Be awake at all moments
to the news that is always
arriving out of the silence.*

Sogyal Rimpoche

Rebirth

Green from the thaw
After winter's icy grey,
Vast, unpeopled spaces greet my eye
As I drive across this landscape
That has become my home.

I used to love autumn best,
When fiery reds and golds
Give one last shout
Before retiring into silence.

But spring calls me now
To welcome possibility,
To don the smile long folded
In a drawer of past delights,
To let the truth of life renewed
Blossom with the promise of summer fruit
And bring me buoyant, dancing joy.

My mind fills up with Nature's pure example,
And I feel my heart's revival,
As over high plains grasslands
Gangly antelope babies run and leap
In the sheer exuberance
Of being born upon the green.

CHAPTER 25

A Gift from the Divine

The Beautiful Middle of Now Here is the gathering point for all of the challenges we have met while traversing the metamorphic spiral. Here we expect miracles, and in this space we find surcease from our labors.

We discover that the razor's edge of change is always growing, expanding outward while going deeper within. We experience greater dimensions of personal freedom and more frequent episodes of inspired creativity.

Receptivity is now our way of life. We have learned to notice bits of resistance and then surrender them to the flame of transformation before they become impediments to progress. Each question becomes its own threshold, each affirmation the beginning of a new conversation with change's eloquent repartée.

A single day's journey through the realm of time and space becomes a vast ocean of experience. Wave upon wave of question and answer caresses the shoreline of consciousness, wearing away boulders of doubt and fear, reducing them to glistening white sands of opportunity.

Here the separation of land and sea and sky melds into a singular landscape upon which we may take inspired and practical action. For the Beautiful Middle of Now Here is nothing if not practical. That is its *raison d'être*. Not to escape the world, but to be sublimely grounded in it.

Like the tip of a spinning top, this is the balance point that functions in perpetual motion, making minute adjustments, remaining upright even in the midst of an ever-changing environment.

Increasingly we merge with the Wise Inner Counselor, the presence we have come to know as our own fully actualized Self. Darkness cannot abide in its light, but we must never take this communion for granted. If we choose to thrive amidst change, then we must daily renew our commitment to the process of self-transcendence.

Each day we are born anew, and with that birth a renewed invitation to embrace wholeness appears. Each day a choice is offered to turn back to safer territory or to accept intensifying rigors. To succumb to a lingering voice of fear or to bravely face our challenges and walk straight into them with hearts wide open.

As long as we live in time and space, obstacles will appear. The path up the mountain of authenticity grows steeper, the potential for slippage more perilous. And still, with greater hardship comes greater reward.

Part Nine: Renaissance - The Beautiful Middle of Now Here

Triumph over adversity evokes tender gratitude when we realize that we of our mere human self did not achieve it alone. Our victories flow from teamwork with unseen helpers who rejoice in a job well done and who relish our conscious acknowledgement of their timely, yet seamless, assistance.

Just as every student has a teacher, every teacher has a Teacher. Every coach has a Coach. Every counselor has a Wise One to whom he or she goes for guidance and perspective. The Universe expands as each traveler internalizes the One who has gone before and then transcends the lessons that were taught from heart to heart.

Like the Phoenix bird that rises from the ashes of its own destruction, in the Beautiful Middle of Now Here our path is one of perpetually re-imagining life's brilliance. In that miraculous unfolding, we are continually reborn.

CHAPTER 26

Be a Traveler, Not a Seeker

At one time or another we are all seekers. Whether our goal is professional success or personal growth, at some point in our lives we will find ourselves perched on a seawall, scanning the horizon, looking for signs of an elusive something.

The problem with seeking is that it means casting about for a thing you do not have. There is a sense of lack or vacancy about it—even despair or sadness, which do disservice to the path of self-realization.

Mariners who sailed these transitory waters before us found the route across. As they made their way through dark seas, they charted a course for others to follow. And they left behind an internal map that is etched in the Spirit-spark that lives in every heart.

The Wise Inner Counselor has direct access to this map. And when our outer awareness is receptive, it is able to convey fragments of it—though rarely all at once.

Part Nine: Renaissance - The Beautiful Middle of Now Here

When we do catch a glimpse, it is only over to the present horizon. Lookouts may spy the voyage's next arc, but no further. We must trust the Unknown to guide us. It is not for the human consciousness to know precisely what's coming; this route is navigated with the heart, not the head.

We are not meant to wrest the guidebook from the Great Mystery. Whether by sea or by land, we must travel in fearless faith, knowing that we will find our next destination without seeking.

As humble sojourners in the care of our Wise Inner Counselor, we find inspiration and direction at every turn. We honor each encounter as a point of wisdom, seeing creative potential in all situations, embracing them as lessons for our highest good.

The key is to rest in gentle recognition of our heart's desire so we will recognize it when it appears. We work hard for its fulfillment but we are never greedy for it. We do not grasp.

We welcome every bend in the road as an adventure. And we greet each fellow traveler as a harbinger of greater truth, or as a reminder to pick up a dropped stitch of consciousness in the great tapestry of Self that we are weaving, strand by golden strand.

The gateway to tomorrow does not swing wide to the demanding gaze. It is the open heart that becomes the passage through to new birth.

To this end, the Wise Inner Counselor offers a key:

Those who choose this path are alert to cosmic signposts left by unseen guides. And yet they journey without expectation.

By leaving behind doubt and a sense of struggle, those who sojourn are not disappointed. They may be challenged by the rigors of the path, but they are also guided, protected, and illumined by whom and what they meet.

Their innocence is their shield. The power of love is their armor. Their receptivity is a sure defense—for their minds detect dangers to avoid, and their hearts read true.

They do not challenge their guides. They simply travel and arrive, perhaps weary, even in grief for the loss of what must fall away as the path grows steeper.

And always do they walk with an intimate awareness that they live in the palm of a divine hand.

CHAPTER 27

Making LIGHT of Change

The Beautiful Middle of Now Here is a place of jubilant personal freedom. Here we transcend the doleful paths of previous traditions.

A brighter way opens before us and the five LIGHT affirmations converge in joyful, creative, ever-unfolding synthesis of all that has gone before. As we have been transformed, so have our expressions of positive affirmation. Until we once more transcend our understanding, they may read:

L   Life on the spiral of change has prepared me for the challenges that will surely come.

I   I practice telling the truth, for my True Self is impeccable.

G   Grounded in my Wise Inner Counselor, I know what I need and what is needed of me.

H   Healing happens when I open up, and heart-centered acceptance heals all wounds.

T   Tomorrow unfolds according to my highest intention.

Making LIGHT of Change

Because we have made this journey with courage and faith, we have emerged from the Middle of Nowhere as a new creature—a better version of our self that is powerfully creative and deeply loving. In the process we find purpose and meaning in life.

In profound awareness of life's unceasing variety, we make LIGHT of change—as radiant acknowledgement that we have walked straight into our challenges, embracing their ambiguity with a willingness to learn from them.

Rather than rushing through transition's discomfort to a safe and familiar pattern of living—one that actually obscures the life our True Self desires—we have lit a candle in the night. With what began as a flicker, we have fanned the flame of resilience, allowing it to transform us even as it has burned away the dross of blind selfishness that, for too long, has kept us limited by the ego's fears.

By making LIGHT of change, we have discovered aspects of our True Self that could only have been uncovered by the dramatic disruption of our contentment. And for this we are eternally grateful.

CHAPTER 28

A Glimpse of Cosmic Purpose

We may never know what an experience is really for until weeks or months or years after the fact. And then, in a flash of insight, we may realize that upsetting the apple cart of certainty was life's most important catalyst for our self-realization.

We have reached a new level of consciousness that is radiant, compassionate, and free. Past, present, and future all converge in the Beautiful Middle of Now Here, where we clearly recognize the breathtaking power of change to propel us out of limited understanding into a more evolved tomorrow that is happening right now.

There is something deeply grounding about this place. It opens up worlds of potential that are practical and precisely applicable to our present circumstance—and which may involve our embarking on another spiral.

The ability to engage in multiple concurrent transitions is what it means to live on the razor's edge—which is really not an edge at all. We may call it a cliff, a threshold, or a frontier; but it is actually that instant just before an edge forms.

Like the hurricane's eye, it is surrounded with edges while not being an edge itself. It is an interval of sublime intention for all that is good and true and beautiful. It is a gap between thought and action—a timeless, formless space into which inspiration may flash.

This cosmic territory is pure potential. And like the Tao, the razor's edge that can be named is not the real one. We can talk about it, but we cannot capture its completeness in words. We can create the environment that it appears to favor, but we cannot force it into existence.

There is much we do not know about it. What we do know is that every razor's edge is unified with every other. And regardless of the particulars, we also know that the real reason for change is always to bring us face to face with the razor's edge.

Becoming Transition Leaders

We travel through life in spurts of genius within a fluid present where all is unlimited love and light. We are meant to internalize the brilliance.

Like adding a golden stone to the edifice of Self or another rung on our ladder of awareness, the idea is for those flashes of insight and connection to become part of us. They become the rule of our being, not the exception.

Part Nine: Renaissance - The Beautiful Middle of Now Here

Living in this flow becomes an art form as we dance with the paradox of destruction and rebirth that is the true essence of life in time and space—and that brings with it both responsibility and reward.

For here we become transition leaders. Whether change has found us or we have pursued it, once we have passed through the thin place that separates Nowhere from Now Here, life will never be the same.

The Beautiful Middle of Now Here is that state of being where we naturally respond appropriately to what is arising. We can now take action anywhere at any time. It is an exhilarating existence.

This Beautiful Middle of Now Here carries within it the call for resilience, hope, and an adventurous, trusting spirit. If we are to go forth in life as agents of positive change, we must take responsibility for our intentions and bend our actions toward the highest good for all.

Here is how the Wise Inner Counselor describes this state of awareness to which we would become increasingly accustomed:

> *These days of dramatic realignment require compassionate, thoughtful, integrated personalities—those who live and work in partnership with Spirit through engaged, purposeful action that flows from refined attunement and wise compassion. These true hearts, lovingly at one with inner guidance, become powerfully effective instruments for positive change. And this is our intention.*

A Glimpse of Cosmic Purpose

The world may be in crisis, but it is not without hope. For as individuals answer the call to personal greatness as co-creators with the Divine, life itself rises up to throw off the seeming chaos of transition's alchemy.

Those who have seen the light are called to share the light, and it is a joyful task. In fact, the nature of those who live in the Beautiful Middle of Now Here is to extend their hearts in loving kindness, perpetually making LIGHT of change for those who would travel this way.

United in love, this activity is what we do best. Together we embrace the flow. Dancing on the spiral of transcendence, we move to the music of cosmic purpose.

And in the process, we find our way home to a glorious future that has always been right here—on the razor's edge of change.

The Catalyst

She was a born change-maker.

Though she meant no harm,
situations and people made major shifts
when she came on the scene;

    and by the time she had moved on,
    no circumstance remained untouched,
        not even the condition
        of her own heart.

For life sent her into strange events
that puzzled her for many years,

    until she came to see the pattern
    of enthusiastic beginnings,
    her being filled with pluck and hope
    for what could be accomplished,
        only to be met with anger,
        stone walls, and rejection
        from those she'd come to help.

In early days an innocence
had encouraged her to sally forth;

    but now when a deeper nature beckoned
    that she should seize a perilous cup,
        her mind recalled in vivid scenes
        the enigma of her lonely path,
        in reluctant recollection
        of the burden she would bear.

For even though she welcomed change
as life's essential principle,
> most folks did not—and blamed her
> for the consequence of their own deeds
>> that her presence
>> had simply brought to light.

She felt self-doubt impeding her path,
and so questioned her ancient mentors.

But these masterful ones,
> from their wiser view,
>> had never found her behavior strange;
>> they cherished her disruptions.

And counted as grace her propensity
> to ignite the fresh enlivening flame
> that rouses those who nap so deep
> they do not care to dream.

For wise ones know from ages past
> that till sleepers finally reconnect
> with their own great master plan,
> there can be no magic in their days
> nor lasting sparkle in their nights.

Someone must summon the winds of change
> to rearrange complacency
> and turn inertia to soulful action
> filled with conscious longing.

And the sages always meant, of course,
    for that someone to be her.

So now, when Fortune calls her name,
the catalyst may sigh aloud
in profoundest human reluctance;
    but she, nevertheless, accepts the task
    to wrestle with the enmity
    of those who in their secret hearts
        yearn to shake off
        the hypnotic trance
        imposed on them
        by a drowsy world
            that fears the soul
            on fire for life.

She lives to learn and love and teach,
    to see the once-dull animate,
    to feel the sudden surge of the few
        who catch the wave
        of her inspiration.

And then she knows her passion's reward,
    as they claim the birthright that is theirs,
    turn back to bid her a grateful farewell,
        and disappear
        bright-eyed for good
            over the horizon
            of their destiny.

START HERE GUIDE

Crisis, either devastating or seemingly minor, can be any event or change that throws you off kilter. The five LIGHT questions in this guide can help you find your balance.

Here are some tips that point the way to your achieving the best results:

- Breathe deeply.
- Take notes on key ideas and inspirations.
- Be patient with yourself.
- Understand that change contains both peaks and valleys.
- Believe that you really can make it through—even beyond this crisis.

START HERE GUIDE

If You're in Crisis Now

To immediately begin implementing The LIGHT Process, read the condensed explanation of each of the five questions in this guide and start the process of inquiry.

Just a suggestion: I have found that it helps to write down both the questions and your answers. Doing so can prompt insights that merely holding concepts in your head does not provide.

I realize that if you are reading this section it is most likely because you are in the midst of change and, therefore, pressed for time. I honor that challenge.

However, let me assure you that my colleagues, my students, and I have discovered that when we write out the details of a situation, very quickly we feel our own commitment to the process of transformation locking in. More often than not, we get impressive results.

Writing down our questions and possible answers opens the floodgates of inspiration, and we are amazed at

Start Here Guide

how much wisdom and insight emerge to support us and resolve our situations.

We have also found that trying to hold insights mentally keeps the conscious mind full, or at least unavailable to receive more. We can only focus on one or two thoughts at a time. Writing down the ideas that naturally begin to flow allows us to remain receptive to additional information. Then we can temporarily let go of what we've written down, because we know we'll be able to review it once the full rush of insights is complete.

This is one of many paradoxes you will encounter on the journey through change. Writing things down may take some time, but the inspirations you get will surely save you time in the long run.

Once your current circumstances allow, I encourage you to return to Parts One through Nine of this work to explore how the affirmations emerge and to get a sense of the transformative experience that change offers. Poems, stories, and nine conceptual themes also provide rich context in which the conversation between question and answer takes place.

As you read through this guide, don't feel bound to follow an exact sequence. Navigating transition is like jumping onto a merry-go-round in motion. When the ride is spinning, you just hop onto the horse in front of you.

If You Are in Crisis Now

Change is not linear. So you can pick up The LIGHT Process wherever it resonates with you and make your way through all five questions from that point forward. The spiraling action of the process will eventually bring you back to the question you started with—now with more self-knowledge, insight, and practical solutions.

Question 1
How have I been prepared?

It's hard to feel prepared when you've been blindsided by a sudden shift in circumstance. When change is planned, it is equally important to establish a baseline from which to innovate.

So the purpose of this question is to help you identify what you know, what you can do, and most importantly—who you are as an individual.

First, write down the basic facts of your situation: What has happened or what do you want to have happen? Then make a list of the knowledge, skills, competencies, innate talents, and positive character traits that you bring to the situation.

If the enormity of either plans or predicaments has overwhelmed you, completing this exercise may allow you to flip the question from *Why me?* to *Why not me?* Sometimes this simple analysis is all you'll need to comprehend your ability to handle a situation that might overwhelm others.

Affirmation 1
Life has prepared me for my current situation.

Question 2
How am I staying afloat?

When you find yourself in the rough waters of change, you must do more than hold your breath until the immediate danger passes. You need some kind of internal life raft.

Many people find that a regular practice such as meditation, centering prayer, or physical exercise helps them weather storms of change—either those imposed from without or those they have initiated.

If you have such a practice, the purpose of this question is to remind you that periods of change are the time to deepen centering practice, not abandon it.

If you do not have a regular practice, my experience with The LIGHT Process suggests that taking even a few minutes a day to be alone, go for a short walk, breathe deeply, and find the rhythm of your own heartbeat can help you stay connected with a sustaining presence of personal integrity that is more powerful than your current dilemma.

Affirmation 2
I practice daily being true to my Self.

Question 3
What do I need right now?

If you are the go-to person for your family, business, or community, your focus is naturally on the needs of others. But, as any caregiver knows, you must periodically replenish your own inner resources or you will have nothing left to offer those who depend on you.

Your ability to determine what you need in the present moment largely depends on how well you can tap into centered, self-reflective awareness.

Your goal at this midpoint of The LIGHT Process is to respond in a proactive manner that supports your True Self, rather than in a reactive way that stems from a fearful, grasping ego.

In the midst of a major transition it may be necessary to push through for a while on little sleep and fast food. But this is not the way to stay strong for the long term. Paying attention to the body's wisdom and your own intuition is the best way to practice self-care that will see you through to change's resolution.

Affirmation 3
Grounded in my body, I know what I need.

Question 4
What do I need to let go of?

As we move through life, it is inevitable that cherished people, possessions, and ideas will pass away. It may be that favorite pastimes, habitual behaviors, or practices that have made you successful in the past are disappearing in favor of the new life that is emerging.

So the purpose of this question is to help you realize that letting go is often the wisest response. Even the most positive of changes can be accompanied by elements of loss and grief. Learning to be open to that likelihood is key.

You may also find that releasing worry and fear will allow good things to come to you, especially as you open up to the opportunities that change has wrought.

Being receptive to fresh perspectives teaches you to let go of that which is already naturally falling away, even as you hold dear what remains useful. In addition to the discovery of brilliant new ideas, deep healing and resolution between individuals and within groups can result.

Affirmation 4
Healing happens when I open up.

Question 5
Where do I go from here?

When you have profoundly engaged in the first four questions, a dazzling, previously unimaginable future may call you forward into a regenerated spirit of hope and creative possibility, carrying you into new and more fruitful spirals of progress.

The key here is to become astutely aware of how you innovate. Intentions matter. Individual thoughts lead to actions that have far-reaching consequences for entire communities and for the world.

So as you reflect upon the journey you have just completed, allow your vision to widen and consider how you might move forward with greater compassion for those who struggle with change. And how you might help others navigate the turbulence from which you have just emerged—after a bit of beach time, of course. Our considerate Universe does honor the importance of self-care.

There are discoveries to be made at the razor's edge. The tomorrow that is calling you forward is richer with potential than you ever imagined possible.

Affirmation 5
Tomorrow unfolds as naturally as I allow.

A BIT OF THIS & THAT
Notes
Acknowledgements
The Conversation Continues

Notes

Chapter 1
1. I highly recommend the books, articles, and video about Rick Rescorla's relentless dedication to his own unique calling of service found on his website at www.RickRescorla.com. James B. Stewart's book *The Heart of a Soldier* (New York: Simon & Schuster, 2003) is recommended, as is Susan Rescorla's memoir *Touched by a Hero*.

    Rescorla's story demonstrates that following inner guidance is not a magical or occasional activity. It demands persistence, courage, and an unflinching determination to refine intuition by learning from one's experience.

Chapter 5
2. John Welwood, *Toward a Psychology of Awakening: Buddhism, Psychotherapy, and the Path of Personal and Spiritual Transformation* (Boston: Shambhala Publications, 2002), p. 11–14.
3. Intuitive life coach Susan Harrow is an expert on vision boards. For more information about her coaching services and to purchase her booklet, *Creating Your Vision with Inspired Intention*, contact her at https://www.LiveLifeVibrant.com.
4. Peter A. Levine, *Waking the Tiger: Healing Trauma* (Berkeley, CA: North Atlantic Books, 1997). Levine quotes Eugene Gendlin, who coined the term. Gendlin defines the *felt sense* as "an internal aura that encompasses everything you feel and know about the given subject at a given time—encompasses it and communicates it to

you all at once rather than detail by detail" (97). Envisioning the felt sense of a desired outcome enhances our ability to manifest it.
5. Dr. Wayne W. Dyer and Eckhart Tolle, *The Importance of Being Extraordinary*, audio CD (Audible audiobook). Dyer gives a full description of the origin of the term "I AM" as the name of God given to Moses in the Book of Exodus (3:14). He and Tolle explain how they use the phrase and concept in their own lives.

Chapter 6
6. For additional information about Levine's work or to locate a somatic therapist, see www.traumahealing.org.

Chapter 7
7. For more about my experiences with the thin places of Ireland, see Cheryl Lafferty Eckl, *A Beautiful Death: Keeping the Promise of Love* (Livingston, MT: Flying Crane Press, 2012), p. 235–50.

Chapter 9
8. I actually experienced a similar life review in a waking state. I had recently sold the home that my late husband and I shared for ten years and where I remained following his death.

  I had occasion to return to the neighborhood and was driving along familiar streets. Suddenly, visions of our experiences from those years flashed before me, as if contained in iridescent globes. This was no mere reminiscence. Each event or life cycle seemed to be playing in its entirety—a bit like a movie trailer.

  As one-by-one these globes passed before my inner sight, I felt a sense of completion and deep gratitude for the amazing experiences that had transpired in that house during the most important period of mental, emotional, and spiritual growth in my life.
9. Adapted from Ned Herrmann's two classic works in Whole Brain® technology: *The Creative Brain* (Lake Lure, NC: Brain Books, 1989) and *The Whole Brain Business Book* (New York: McGraw-Hill, 2015).

Chapter 11
10. Linda Kohanov, *The Tao of Equus: A Woman's Journey of Healing and Transformation through the Way of the Horse* (Novato, CA: New World Library, 2001), p. 32–33.

Chapter 14

11. See https://www.noirin.love for Nóirín Ní Ríain's biography, discography, and upcoming events.
12. The term *fractal*, derived from the Latin word *fractus* ("fragmented" or "broken"), was coined by the Polish-born mathematician Benoit B. Mandelbrot, who developed the Mandelbrot set—a simple mathematical equation involving complex numbers.

    Fractals are objects that appear to be like each other at various scales. Magnifying a fractal reveals small-scale details similar to the large-scale characteristics. However, the small-scale details are not identical to the whole.

    Like a Mandelbrot set, The LIGHT Process is a self-referencing system. It uses the output of one spiral as the input for the next, adding its own creative spin to the sum of the previous whole to create a new similar, but unique, whole.

    The concept resonates with Ken Wilber's idea of *holons*—a concept explained by the sequence of letters to words to phrases to sentences to paragraphs to chapters to books to libraries. Each piece is a whole and is also part of a more complex whole.

Chapter 15

13. According to Aeschylus's tragedy *Agamemnon*, Cassandra was loved by the god Apollo, who promised her the power of prophecy if she would comply with his desires. Cassandra accepted the proposal, received the gift, and then refused the god her favors. Apollo revenged himself by ordaining that her prophecies should never be believed. She accurately predicted such events as the fall of Troy and the death of Agamemnon, but her warnings went unheeded.
14. *dan tien* (Chinese, "elixir field"). For a clear explanation and experiential exploration of this life force center, see Terrence Dunn's classic DVD, *T'ai Chi for Health: Yang Long Form* (Koch Studio, 2004).
15. Somatic awareness is critical to the journey through change. In 1983 Dr. Howard Gardner from Harvard University identified bodily-kinesthetic intelligence as one of the primary ways in which human beings interact with the world.

    The work of Dr. Dawna Markova provides practical keys to accessing bodily-kinesthetic intelligence. See *The Open Mind: Exploring the Six Patterns of Natural Intelligence* (Boston: Conari Press, 1996).

My experience with adult learners has clearly demonstrated that many people would find greater satisfaction in work and life if they understood the power of body wisdom. Opening to somatic experience is especially applicable to the journey through change.

Chapter 16

16. William Wordsworth, *Lines Written a Few Miles above Tintern Abbey, on Revisiting the Banks of the Wye during a Tour, July 13, 1798*.

Chapter 17

17. I have been asked, "If the Wise Inner Counselor is so great, why didn't it prevent the accident?" My answer is that sometimes events have to happen. We may need the lesson the experience offers. The event may be necessary for the blessings that will follow. In my case, I believe that my being in a serious car accident had been postponed years earlier. When it eventually transpired, the severity had been mitigated by my years of prayer and spiritual discipline. These are things we will never know for certain in this life.

Chapter 18

18. For a complete exposition on the critical process of reconstructing meaning in bereavement, see editor and contributor Robert A. Neimeyer's *Meaning Reconstruction and the Experience of Loss* (Washington, DC: American Psychological Association, 2001).

Chapter 19

19. Edison was known to take afternoon catnaps on his rolltop desk. Napping was one of his "methods for balancing intensity and relaxation." Michael J. Gelb and Sarah Miller Caldicott, *Innovate Like Edison: The Success System of America's Greatest Inventor* (New York: Dutton, 2007), hardbound, p. 117.

Chapter 20

20. See https://www.MysticalArtsofTibet.org for examples of sand paintings and of how Tibetan monks produce them.
21. Jamie Sams and David Carson, *Medicine Cards: The Discovery of Power Through the Ways of Animals*, revised, expanded edition (New York: St. Martin's Press, 1999), p. 142.

22. Elizabeth Lesser, *Broken Open: How Difficult Times Help Us Grow* (New York: Villard Books, 2005), p. 273.
23. I have found that writing poetry is a powerful and enjoyable tool for working with otherwise submerged thoughts and feelings. (See https://www.CherylEckl.com/books/)

Chapter 21

24. Eckl, *A Beautiful Death*.

Chapter 22

25. Sogyal Rimpoche, *Tibetan Wisdom for Living and Dying*, (Available on Audible audiobooks).
26. Dame Cicely Saunders, who founded the modern hospice movement in the UK in the early 1970s, said, "You matter because you are." Her compassionate dedication to easing the suffering of other human beings has been a profound inspiration in my own work.
27. The way I heard the story, my father learned military radio technology from the Signal Corps and then worked for the Army Air Corps. Officially, the Air Corps became a subordinate element of the Army Air Forces on June 20, 1941, and was abolished as an administrative organization during General George C. Marshall's reorganization of 1942, when it became a combat arm of the Army Air Forces.

Chapter 23

28. This comment speaks to the concept of why bad things happen to good people. For a brilliant exploration of this question, see Harold S. Kushner, *When Bad Things Happen to Good People* (New York: Anchor Books, 2004). Rabbi Kushner's assertion is that God is not in control of what happens in time and space. However, the Divine is always present as the source of comfort, unique solutions, and profound personal transformation.

Chapter 24

29. Jack H. Engler, "Becoming Somebody and Nobody: Psychoanalysis and Buddhism," in *Paths Beyond Ego: The Transpersonal Vision*, Roger Walsh, M.D., Ph.D., and Frances Vaughan, Ph.D., eds. (Los Angeles: Jeremy P. Tarcher/Perigee, 1993), p. 119.

Acknowledgements

This book would have been much more challenging to write without the loving support of dear friends and colleagues, Mimi, Kathleen, Evelyn, Susan, Scott, and Andres, who provided hospitality and insights that supported and inspired me in countless ways.

Special thanks are due to Irene, Sam, Gretchen, and Chuck—not their real names, of course—and to Paul for lending me your stories. And deep gratitude to colleagues Theresa McNicholas, James Bennett and Olivia Hoyt who exhibited enormous fortitude and resilience during the production process.

My heart overflows with gratitude to my own Wise Inner Counselor, to Stephen and my many extraordinary teachers. You have placed your faith in me and you have never left my side. May we continue to meet at the razor's edge in ever-deepening exploration of change's creative spirals. I am yours forever.

The Conversation Continues with the Wise Inner Counselor™

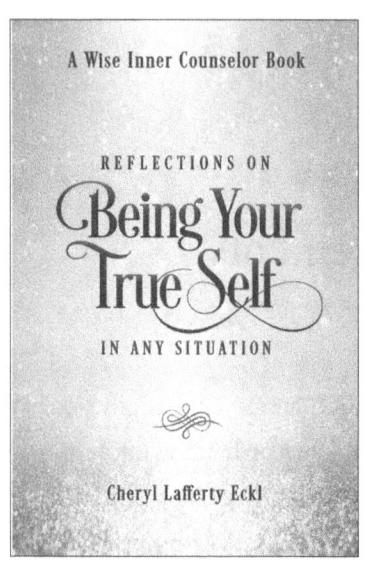

Have you ever longed for a friend who loves you unconditionally?

Such a friend exists within you as the powerful voice of inner guidance, known as your Wise Inner Counselor or True Self.

When you partner with this voice of limitless creativity, love and compassion, it will skillfully guide you through a world dizzied by the accelerating pace of ever-changing events.

164 pages   ISBN: 978-1-7367123-0-6

What makes your work great and you great at work?

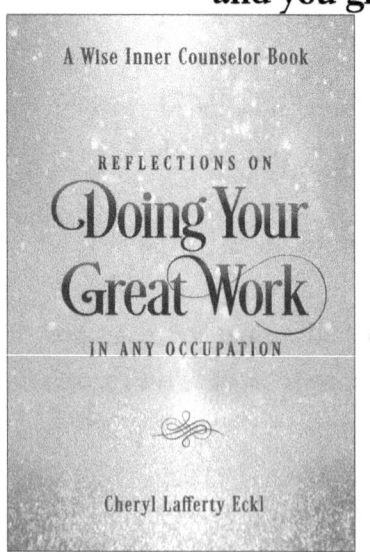

Cheryl Lafferty Eckl has spent many years pondering those questions. Now, for the first time in print, she shares her reflections on the timeless principles, behaviors and attitudes that can help you become highly effective in any occupation.

She invites you to unlock your wise inner voice and discover within your own heart the real secret to fulfilling your personal greatness.

166 pages   ISBN: 978-1-7367123-2-0

More from the Wise Inner Counselor™

Reflections on Ineffable Love: from loss through grief to joy

Love Is Stronger Than Death

While I navigated the rough waters of grief after the passing of my husband and twin flame, Stephen, many experiences proved to me that love is not only stronger than death, love transcends death.

During the worst event of my life, I made an amazing discovery. Although Stephen was no longer alive on earth, our souls could communicate through the veil that separates this world and the next.

More than thirteen years after my beloved lifted off for other realms, our sacred love tryst grows stronger every day. Through inspirational stories, meditations and poetry, I am grateful to offer you my reflections on this unique path we are blessed to walk.

For I have come to know that...
>loss is for our learning,
>grief is for our transformation,
>and joy is eager to bring us Home to our soul,
>our twin flame and our True Self.

Cheryl Lafferty Eckl

198 pages * ISBN: 978-1-7346450-9-5

Returning

Each new passage is a walk into darkness.

Opportunity beckons again,
But you can only hear her knock
At a threshold you've already crossed.

Since early childhood, Cheryl has had a zest for life. As a singer and actress, she used her dramatic and comedic skills to delight musical theater audiences across the U.S.

When she turned her attention to helping others as a professional development trainer and life transitions facilitator, a new audience was equally receptive—this time to her knowledge and unique insights into life's changes.

Cheryl has delivered her practical wisdom with intelligence, humor, and real-life stories for many years and has trained top performers in a variety of industries. She lives in Livingston, Montana, where big skies and lofty mountains inspire her path through change with her own Wise Inner Counselor.

Learn more at www.CherylEckl.com.

www.ingramcontent.com/pod-product-compliance
Lightning Source LLC
Chambersburg PA
CBHW051428290426
44109CB00016B/1473